Gareth Owen is a retired qualifications development manager, lecturer, tutor and researcher in accountancy and finance and is an experienced author of accounting and finance teaching and curricula materials.

Gareth has a BA(Hons) in Accountancy and Finance from Lancaster University, an MBA from the University of Wales and an MPhil by research in finance, from the Open University.

His main research interests have been in the decomposition and valuation of goodwill, shareholder value added, integrated reporting and the determination of the cost of capital. He has also published a student text book on accounting, contributed chapters and reviews to other academic publications and has written several articles to support student learning and the understanding of key study and revision principles in professional accountancy.

The book is the result of many years of thought and research into the cost of capital question and is a personal summary of these findings. However, my inspirations for the thinking have originally come from such eminent authors as John Burr Williams and Modigliani and Miller, where the fundamental concepts of capital structure irrelevance were first addressed.

Another key author who needs a special mention is Stewart Myers (1974) for his elegant simplification of the cost of capital problem, with the adjusted present value formula, which I have adapted and rearranged in this book as a simple and flexible way of valuing a company or additional investments, where constant growth and taxation need to be accounted for.

Gareth Owen

The Cost of Capital and Company Valuation

Modigliani and Miller Revisited

Austin Macauley Publishers

LONDON * CAMBRIDGE * NEW YORK * SHARJAH

Copyright © Gareth Owen 2025

The right of Gareth Owen to be identified as author of this work has been asserted by the author in accordance with sections 77 and 78 of the Copyright, Designs and Patents Act 1988.

All rights reserved. No part of this publication may be reproduced, stored in a retrieval system, or transmitted in any form or by any means, electronic, mechanical, photocopying, recording, or otherwise, without the prior permission of the publishers.

Any person who commits any unauthorised act in relation to this publication may be liable to criminal prosecution and civil claims for damages.

A CIP catalogue record for this title is available from the British Library.

ISBN 9781035871667 (Paperback)
ISBN 9781035871674 (ePub e-book)

www.austinmacauley.com

First Published 2025
Austin Macauley Publishers Ltd®
1 Canada Square
Canary Wharf
London
E14 5AA

I would very much like to thank Austin Macauley Publishers for taking a serious interest in this book when first submitted to them and for giving it such a detailed review. This review gave me the confidence to enter into a partnership with them to produce this publication.

I would also like to thank former colleagues and fellow researchers, who are too many to mention, for patiently listening to me and in some cases possibly misunderstanding me, when I was trying to explain my major propositions.

I would also like to thank my former MPhil supervisor from the Open University, Professor Janette Rutterford, for inspiring me to think more deeply about this subject and for sowing some interesting seeds of thought in my mind.

Finally, I would like to thank my wife, Julie, for her support and our young grandchildren, Dylarah, Nate and Ottilie, for allowing me enough free time to finalise this work and get it ready for publication.

Table of Contents

Foreword	11
Abstract	15
Introduction	16
Chapter 1: Modigliani and Miller and the 'World Without Taxes'	18
Chapter Summary	32
Chapter 2: How the Modigliani and Miller Propositions Explain the Relationship Between Ke_g and Gearing	34
Chapter Summary	40
Chapter 3: Modigliani and Miller and the 'World with Taxes'	41
Chapter Summary	53
Chapter 4: Growth Assumptions	55
Chapter Summary	59
Chapter 5: The Company-Wide Cost of Capital As a 'Hurdle Rate' for Additional Project or Investment Appraisal	61
Chapter Summary	64
Chapter 6: Valuing Additional Projects or Investments	65
Chapter Summary	74
Chapter 7: The Effect of Gearing on the Company-Wide and Project-Specific Costs of Equity Capital (Ke_g) and WACC	76
Chapter Summary	78

Chapter 8: Valuing Companies When the Additional Investment, Project or Division Has a Different Asset Beta from That of the Company As a Whole   79

Chapter Summary   83

Chapter 9: Additional 'What-If' Scenarios Relating to the Additional Investment   84

Chapter Summary   93

Chapter 10: Negative Cash Flows   95

Chapter Summary   101

Chapter 11: Implications of the Above Analysis for Valuing Companies and Investment Projects   102

Chapter Summary   104

Chapter 12: Conclusions   105

Bibliography   108

Postscript How to Value a Company: A Step-by-Step Methodology   110

Foreword

Since I was an accounting and finance undergraduate at Lancaster University in the 1970s, I have wondered about the purpose and relevance of the 'weighted average cost of capital' in terms of shareholder value and valuing companies. I started to think about this further when I was teaching an ACCA final professional-level class in the late 1980s about FRS 4 'Capital Instruments', well before the treatment of financial instruments and leases became a much more developed topic, both in the UK and internationally.

Generally accepted accounting practice recommends that however a bond or security is sold and packaged as a financial instrument, whether redeemable or irredeemable, whatever its coupon rate of interest, whether it is deep-discounted on sale or redemption, it always has an implicit financial cost, namely the price of borrowing to the company, or more specifically its shareholders. This implicit cost to the company is inclusive of the required rate of return of the lenders. Furthermore, from the shareholders' own perspective, using that implicit cost as a rate to discount the net cash flows associated with the security or financial instrument yields a zero net present value for that security, at any point during the repayment period.

Almost all instructional finance books and so many academic papers I have read, from so many sources, developing so many valuation paradigms, often refer to the 'weighted average cost of capital' (WACC) as the universal metric for estimating the opportunity cost facing a company's investors.

The cost of financing a geared company is explained as a blend of the cost of equity and the cost of borrowing, adjusted for the capital structure. There is a presumed 'capital pool' where the financial capital of a company is contributed by both owners and lenders—particularly when the cost of capital is considered. This book explains how WACC is a problematic metric in the valuation of companies, and to calculate it as a discount factor to value projects, investments or acquisitions involves a circularity of argument, as it is necessary to know the present value of a company, including its equity to calculate WACC and then use it to value companies or investments. In this book, through some simple re-arrangements of generally known valuation formulae, a more direct but quite differently constructed equation can be developed, which can be used for valuing companies as a whole and, perhaps more importantly, for validly appraising the viability of additional capital investments.

My thinking has always started with considering the agency relationship. When discounting future cash flows, I kept asking myself: *What is the real opportunity cost of investing as far as the shareholders themselves are concerned?*

To answer this question, I asked myself the following about a company:

- *Who invests in the company, and whose capital is it?*
- *Who ultimately obtains a financial return from it?*
- *Who bears the risks involved, and how are these risks compensated for?*
- *Is the cost of capital really a cost to shareholders, or is it their rate of return?*

I have tried to answer these questions in turn.

Who invests in the company, and whose capital is it?

It can always be argued that a range of stakeholders invest in a company, but the cost of the investment to most of these stakeholders such as customers, suppliers, employees, managers, the government and ultimately the taxpayer is never factored into the cost of 'financial capital'. These costs are treated as normal business expenses or cash outflows, where such costs are tangible enough to be recognised and measured. None of these ('third-party') costs are treated as a component of the cost of financial capital. From the traditional 'agency' perspective, it can be argued that direct investment in the financial capital of the company is made exclusively by the 'principals' or shareholders, and the board of directors act as 'agents' to manage this fund on their behalf, transacting with 'third parties', including lenders.

There are, however, good corporate socio-economic arguments to suggest that a variety of capitals of the company are contributed—by a much wider range of stakeholders, but from the financial perspective, the key capital component is the equity investment. Considering financial capital in isolation, the question arises whether the cost of debt should be incorporated within the cost of the financial capital of the company when lenders can be argued as being another albeit important third-party stakeholder. Lenders could be defined as suppliers to the company in the same way that any other supplier of capital is paid a price compensating them for their risk, imputed in their required return. In other words, are the costs of borrowing any different from the costs of employing people, renting property, purchasing inventory or paying insurance premiums or taxes?

Who ultimately obtains the financial return from the company?

Most stakeholders are rewarded for their investment, or they would not invest. Customers receive value for money for the goods and services they purchase; suppliers are paid a fair price for their products and services, including their profit margin; and employees of the company are remunerated for their technical, managerial and intellectual skills and for their physical effort and time. The government and the wider public benefit from the employment and wealth created: lenders receive interest on their loans and the owners take what is left. And this is the point. The owners are the investors who take what is left (if there is any), and the cost of obtaining what is left includes rewarding all other stakeholders who supply their various forms of capital to the company, including lenders. What is left is shareholder return.

Who bears the risk, and how is this compensated for?

So, a range of stakeholders bears the risk in supplying their six capitals (Owen, 2013) to the company, and all charge a price that includes a premium for accepting that risk, as determined by the market conditions and the interaction between the supply of and demand for those capitals. Customers will only pay a price that is reasonable for the product or service offered as compared with alternatives; suppliers face a risk of late payment and default and charge a price for their products and services that will reflect this risk; and employees accept a market rate for their labour, skills and intellect based on the value represented by that service. They are also compensated for unsociable hours or any hazard involved in the work. The rate of pay is the price representing the opportunity cost of offering their labour to an alternative employer where risks may be fewer and security greater and where professional fulfilment and working conditions may be better.

Governments invest in national and human assets and in the infrastructure, incurring financial costs and accepting other risks on behalf of the taxpayer. To compensate for this, they levy taxes on profits, on employment and on any adverse environmental impacts. Lenders receive interest at such a rate, which compensates them for the opportunity cost of deferring their consumption (time value of money) and against the risk of default.

Is the cost of capital really a cost to shareholders, or is it their rate of return?

The term 'cost of capital' may be a misnomer. What remains after the shareholders in the company have rewarded all other suppliers of capital, including compensating them all for the risks that they all face, is their own 'internal rate of return'. In real terms, this rate of return is quantified as the free or residual cash flow available to shareholders after rewarding all the other stakeholders and is a measure of compensation that is to cover all the costs they have incurred and the risks accepted, in making their financial investment. This residual is not a shared cost or return, nor can it be weighted to recognise that others share in it. It is a single, unitary measure of risk or return, available for this particular stakeholder, namely the equity investor.

The short book that follows builds its arguments on the answers given to these fundamental questions of agency about the nature of business capital, specifically financial capital.

Gareth Owen (January 2025)

Abstract

The finance literature contains a considerable amount of research about the appropriate valuation metrics to use in company and project valuation. Much attention in academic and professional journals is focused on the weighted average cost of capital that this book demonstrates is mathematically an irrelevance and involves a circularity of argument.

This book examines the relationship between net cash flows, finance costs/benefits and equity risk from the fundamental principles established by Modigliani and Miller under the assumption of perpetuity, to simplify the proofs. An alternative mathematical formula for calculating the appropriate economic discount or 'hurdle' rate to apply to company valuation or to project or investment appraisal is then demonstrated. The formula can be used to calculate equity stock yield without the need for modification, even when business taxes are payable. This book also demonstrates a straightforward and intuitively logical method to value a project or company when the equity beta and projected cash flows, including interest, tax and outstanding debt, can be estimated. The formula derived in this book gives the most direct relationship between the ungeared cost of capital and company value based on a modified form of the 'adjusted present value' (APV) method.

The book explains, through one continuous illustrative example, how the APV, the weighted average cost of capital (WACC) and the equity valuation (EV) methods can all be used with the appropriate discount rates to value companies and additional investments with consistent results, but using WACC creates a circularity argument, meaning that other methods are preferable.

The book also explains that both the APV and EV methods offer more direct approaches to company valuation than the WACC method, but the EV method gives much clearer signals to the 'agents' or managers of a company about the cost of capital it bears (or return it generates) to compensate its shareholders adequately for risk. Finally, as a postscript to this book, there is a step-by-step approach to the valuation of a company, based on the arguments put forward in this publication.

Introduction

This book considers valuation fundamentals originating from the *Law of the Conservation of Investment Value* (Williams, 1938) and refers to the Modigliani and Miller (M+M) propositions. It applies these to company valuation, using three closely related approaches. These are the 'adjusted present value (APV) method' (Myers, 1974), 'the weighted average cost of capital' (WACC) method (Miles and Ezzell, 1980(a)) and the 'equity valuation' (EV) method, which is essentially a restatement and simplification of the WACC method.

The book demonstrates that because the net present value to the company of all debt instruments, including all forms of lease finance (ignoring any tax benefits that belong exclusively to equity shareholders), is zero by definition, it is possible to simplify the integral relationships between the alternative equity valuation approaches. From that, an alternative mathematical formula for calculating the correct economic discount or 'hurdle' rate to apply to company valuation or to project or investment appraisal can be proved. The same formula can be used without modification, whether business taxes are payable or not. This book shows that this formula and Modigliani and Miller's unmodified formula for calculating the yield on equity capital gives the same result regardless of whether taxation is payable despite the fact that they themselves stated on p. 439 and in equation (12.c) that a modification of their original formula for taxes was necessary (Modigliani and Miller, 1963).

The book revisits the fundamental propositions of Modigliani and Miller in a 'world without taxes', illustrating how all three methods can be entirely consistent in determining corporate value under these assumptions. The book then proceeds to show how valuations arrived at under these alternative approaches remain consistent, even in a 'world with taxes', and that value invariance continues to apply in a 'world with taxes' when the present value of taxation and an adjustment for constant growth is included in the valuation paradigm.

It is concluded that the 'EV' method demonstrated in this book, originally alluded to by Durand (1959), is the most relevant metric for shareholders, as it yields a single rate of return for the geared capital of the company based on forecast net cash flows, accounting for all market risk, financing costs and tax effects.

However, it is also shown that the modified APV formula is by far the most direct method to value companies and because, as it is based on the ungeared cost of equity, it is a much simpler and more concise way to account for debt, taxation and constant growth.

For the purposes of explaining the main proposition in this book, in accordance with Williams (op. cit) and Modigliani and Miller (1961), dividend policy is considered irrelevant, and the displacement property of dividends (Ohlson, 1995) is also assumed whilst accepting that there has long been a longstanding academic debate about the 'signalling' property of dividends in respect of valuation. (Fama, 1974)

Chapter 1
Modigliani and Miller and the 'World Without Taxes'

Modigliani and Miller (M+M), in their capital structure irrelevance theorem (1958), propose that in a 'world without taxes', the value of a geared company should be the same as the value of an ungeared company, regardless of the gearing level of that company. John Burr Williams (1938) in his *Law of the Conservation of Investment Value* seems to have first addressed this ('and possibly the displacement property of dividends') when he explained that the enterprise value (of stocks and bonds) is unaffected by the company's 'capitalisation', which is the term he uses for the financial structure. The key quote is as follows:

> Clearly if a single individual or institutional investor owned all the bonds, stocks and warrants issued by a corporation, it would not matter to this investor what the company's capitalisation rate was[21]. Any earnings collected as interest could not be collected as dividends. To such an individual it would be perfectly obvious that the total interest and dividend paying power was in no wise dependent on the kind of securities issued to the company's owner. Furthermore, no change in the investment value of the enterprise as a whole would result from a change in the capitalisation. (Williams, 1938, pp. 72–73)

[21]Except for details concerning income tax

This quote and (interestingly) the footnote both seem to pre-empt the 'capital structure irrelevance' theory, which was subsequently proposed by Modigliani and Miller, as it is clearly noted that the law only applies in a 'world without taxes'.

Modigliani and Miller, however, explained this 'law' rather differently and proposed that any value premium to be gained in a 'geared' company of a certain class, compared to equivalent 'ungeared' investments in the same asset class would be eroded through 'arbitrage'. This means that the value of the firm in a particular class would be unaffected by any change in gearing when shares and debt instruments can be exchanged freely in an efficient (perfect) market (Proposition 1), and they describe it as follows:

> The market value of the firm is independent of its capital structure and is given by capitalising its expected return at the rate p_k appropriate to its class.
> That is, the average cost of capital, to any firm is completely independent of its capital structure and is equal to the capitalisation rate of a pure equity stream of its class. (Modigliani and Miller, 1958, p. 268)[1]

Modigliani and Miller also analogise Williams' quote above as follows when they describe the present value of the firm as the value of milk, which can be separated into butter fat and skimmed milk:

> Our Proposition 1 states that a firm cannot reduce the cost of capital i.e., increase the market value of the stream it generates by securing part of its capital through the sale of bonds, even though debt money appears to be cheaper. This assertion is equivalent to the proposition that, under perfect markets, a dairy farmer cannot in general earn more for the milk he produces by skimming some of the butter fat and selling it separately, even though butter fat per unit weight, sells for more than whole milk. The advantage from skimming the milk rather than selling whole milk would be purely illusory; for what would be gained from selling the high-priced butter fat would be lost in selling the low-priced residue of thinned milk. (Modigliani and Miller, 1958, pp. 278–279)

M+M are therefore confirming Williams' view that however, the present value of the company is financed; whether entirely by debt or equity or any combination thereof, the value of the company will not be affected, where there are no taxes to consider.

Illustrative example:

Details of a fictitious limited company (Company A) are given below that will be used as the basis of all calculations, which follow, and will be used throughout the rest of this book:

- Invested equity capital = $1m at $1 per share = e
- Value of outstanding debt (irredeemable) = $1m = d
- Ungeared cost of equity capital = 10% = Ke_U
- Geared cost of equity capital to be established = Ke_g
- Weighted average cost of capital to be established = WACC
- Present value of the company to be established = PV_C
- Present value of equity to be established (PV_C - d) = PV_e
- Net present value of equity to be established (PV_e - e) = NPV_e
- Cost of debt (7%) = K_d
- Annual gross cash flows before interest and tax into perpetuity = $300,000 = c
- Business tax rate = 30% = t_R

The members of Company A originally faced a financing decision. Their capital requirements were exactly $2m, and they needed to decide how much they would borrow and how much they would initially invest themselves. This decision involved selecting from a combination of equity or loan funds ranging from one extreme to another. The investors could have decided to invest all $2m themselves or borrow various amounts up to as much as the total cost of the investment. The latter of these extremes is an alternative legal arrangement to that of a conventional limited company, as theoretically, it would represent a type of non-stock company. Such a company could also be formed under certain conditions as a 'company limited by guarantee'.

As can be seen from the data given above, the shareholders of Company A eventually decided to invest $1m themselves and borrow the other $1m, effectively giving their company a nominal gearing of 50%.

Modigliani and Miller and capital structure irrelevance

As stated earlier, M+M proposed that where there are no taxes to consider, the value of the ungeared company should be the same as the value of the geared company or be independent of its capital structure, meaning that the weighted average cost of capital (WACC) remains constant at all levels of gearing. The implications of this proposition are that in these circumstances, WACC must always be the same as the ungeared cost of equity, based on the asset beta.

Calculating the present value of the company (PV$_C$)

The fundamental valuation equations below show that the present value of the company as a whole (including debt), as a perpetuity, can be expressed in two different but equivalent ways, based on Modigliani and Miller's Proposition 1; where in a 'world without taxes', Ke_U = WACC at all levels of gearing:

$$PVc = \frac{c}{Ke_U} \qquad (1)$$

In Equation (1), Ke_u is the same as the capitalisation rate p_k from M+M's Proposition 1, and the equation is the root of the adjusted present value (APV) method without the tax shield adjustment, where the present value of the company (PV$_C$) is the cash flow before interest divided by the ungeared cost of equity.

$$PVc = \frac{c}{WACC} \qquad (2)$$

Equation (2) is a summarised form of the WACC valuation method, or as Modigliani and Miller referred to it, the 'average cost of capital', where the present value of the company (PV$_C$) is equal to the cash flow before interest divided by the WACC. In both cases, it can be seen that the present value of the company as a whole is:

300,000/0.1 = $3,000,000
which by implication consists of the following elements:
Present value of equity = $2,000,000

(The above is broken down to: $1,000,000 being the nominal value of equity and $1,000,000 being the net present value (NPV) of equity.)

Present value of debt = $1,000,000

Modigliani and Miller proposed that Ke_U was calculated as the annual cash flow available to debt and equity holders, divided by the present value of the company, or Equation (1), rearranged as:

$$Ke_U = \frac{c}{PVc}$$

The formula for calculating the WACC is traditionally represented as follows, using the notation given above:

$$WACC = \left(\frac{e}{v} \times Ke_g\right) + \left(\frac{d}{v} \times K_d\right)$$

where $v = PVc$

For a constant perpetuity, this can then be restated as follows:

$$WACC = \left(\frac{c - (d \times K_d)}{PVc}\right) + \left(\frac{d \times K_d}{PVc}\right)$$

Where c - (d x K_d), being the annual cash inflow net of interest, = e x Ke_g

This expanded formula can then be restated and simplified to prove Modigliani's proposition that at all levels of gearing, the WACC always equals Ke_U as follows:

By combining the fractions with a common denominator (PVc), the equation becomes:

$$WACC = \frac{(c - (d \times K_d)) + (d \times K_d)}{PVc}$$

By summing the (d x K_d) elements, the equation can be simplified as follows:

WACC=c/(PVc) which proves that WACC = Ke_U

In effect, this restatement of the WACC formula and simplifying it provides a straightforward proof of Modigliani and Miller's Proposition 1 that at all levels of financial gearing WACC = Ke_U, and because that is true, any change in the amount or cost of debt cannot affect the overall value of a company and ensures 'value invariance'.

Calculating the present value of equity (PV_e)

Adapting Equations (1) and (2) shows that the present value of the company's equity is simply determined by subtracting the nominal value of outstanding debt from the two equations as shown below:

$$PVe = \frac{c}{Ke_U} - d \qquad (3)$$

$$PVe = \frac{c}{WACC} - d \qquad (4)$$

It is assumed, in this illustrative example, that the Ke_U rate is already known. In practice, this would need to be estimated from an empirical measurement of the covariance of past returns to equity shareholders of the company to derive the equity beta. It is then usual for analysts to ungear the equity beta by using the following equation:

$$Ungeared\ beta = \frac{Geared\ beta}{1 + (1 - t_R) \times \frac{debt}{equity}}$$

The calculated 'asset' beta can then be included within the capital asset pricing model CAPM (Treynor, 1961 and Sharpe, 1964) to find the ungeared cost of equity. However, there are problems associated with this, and these will be referred to below, and an alternative methodology is recommended.

The 'baseline' discount rate is the key to the valuation process, as it comprises the systematic and unsystematic risk of the company in its market (Markowitz, 1952) where the latter is assumed not to be diversified within a portfolio of assets but excludes the risk due to financial gearing. It is uncertainty in establishing this which is at the root of all valuation problems, even before cash forecasting can be undertaken, which itself is a subjective process. As mentioned earlier, estimating the ungeared cost of capital is normally achieved by ungearing the equity beta and then using the ungeared beta in the CAPM equation to determine the ungeared cost of capital.

The problem with this formulation, if the objective is to determine the intrinsic value of the company, is that the present value of equity must already be known in order to do this, which creates a circularity problem. The only reasonable figure, which can be used to do this, is the current reported market value of the company, which may be over or undervalued against its intrinsic or fundamental value. The alternative method is to use the already calculated geared or equity beta in the CAPM equation to calculate the geared cost of equity and then to ungear this directly, to find the ungeared cost of capital. The method for doing this will be covered later in the chapter.

Calculating the net present value of debt, using the implicit cost of debt from the shareholders' perspective

Before the relationships between Equations 3 and 4 are examined further, it is worth making a key point, which to date seems not to be evident in much of the finance literature, concerning the value of debt as far as the company itself is concerned, or more specifically to its shareholders, which is the fundamental mathematical basis for Propositions 1 and 2.

From the lenders' perspective, the net present value of the loan made to Company A will be determined by the amount and length of the loan and the difference between the lending and borrowing rates, net of other operating costs, discounted by the lender's own cost of capital. A profitable lender will be earning a positive NPV on its loan book overall. However, from the borrower's or, more specifically, the shareholders' perspective, the NPV of debt, using the implicit discount rate, as recommended in generally accepted accounting principles (GAAP) and, as charged to the equity shareholders by the lenders, must be zero.

It therefore has a completely neutral effect in a company valuation model when tax effects are ignored. The following is the net present value formula for a perpetual debt instrument:

NPV (debt) = ((d x K_d)/K_d) - d, which of course mathematically cancels to zero.[1]

Taking the data from the illustration given above, the NPV of the perpetual debt is confirmed as being zero as follows:

NPV (debt) = (d x Kd)/K_d - d = 70,000/0.07 - 1,000,000 = $0

Using the implicit interest rate (rather than the coupon rate) to discount the finance costs and subtract the outstanding value of debt therefore yields a 'zero' NPV from the company's perspective. This also applies to any debt instrument, including financial leases, at any stage within the repayment period. This therefore means that the 'net present value' of a company is exclusively shareholder value.

Therefore, from an agency perspective, borrowing funds should be seen simply as a third-party transaction such as any other business transaction undertaken by the company on behalf of its shareholders.

In this example, as it is assumed that Ke_U is already known, the present value of the ungeared company's equity can be calculated directly by using the APV formulation in Equation (3) as follows:

PV_e = c/Ke_U - d
= (300,000/0.1) - 1,000,000 = $2,000,000.

---

[1] *This also shows why, unequivocally, the 'capital structure irrelevance theorem' holds* – this is why changes in the amount or cost of debt can never affect company valuation in a 'world without taxes' and why Propositions 1 and 2 apply.

Simplifying the WACC valuation formula

Returning to Equation (4), it is possible to expand that equation as follows because PV_e calculated under the weighted average cost of capital method is essentially decomposed into two separate elements: (i) interest divided by implicit cost of debt to the shareholders and (ii) cash flow less interest divided by the cost of equity, less the value of outstanding debt. This is shown Equation (5):

$$PVe = \left(\frac{d \times K_d}{K_d}\right) + \left(\frac{c - (d \times K_d)}{K_{eg}}\right) - d \qquad (5)$$

Given that $((d \times K_d)/K_d) - d$ is always zero as far as the company is concerned, as discussed above, it can be confirmed that the debt and finance components can be cancelled out from the right-hand side of the equation, meaning that the original Equation 4 can be simplified and restated as Equation 6:

$$PVe = \frac{c - (d \times K_d)}{K_{eg}} \qquad (6)$$

The above simplification of the expanded WACC valuation equation can be simply renamed as the 'equity valuation' (EV) method. Therefore, restating Equation (6), the fundamental cost of capital K_{eg} can be calculated as follows:

$$Ke_g = \frac{c - (d \times K_d)}{PVe} \qquad (7)$$

In the illustrative example given earlier, with annual cash flows (c) being $300,000, the present value of the company (PV_C) will be (300,000/0.1) or $3,000,000 and this remains constant regardless of the capital structure chosen by the members of the company. Therefore, PV_e will be $PV_C - d$ at each level of gearing.

As already stated, the original financing decision involved choosing between various combinations of nominal equity and debt, from where equity is $2m and debt zero to where equity is zero and debt $2m and where the decision was to finance the company equally with debt and equity in monetary terms. However, if the various possible combinations of debt and equity are shown in increments of $200,000, from one extreme to the other, the Ke_g and WACC (WACC) can be graphically presented in Figure 1:

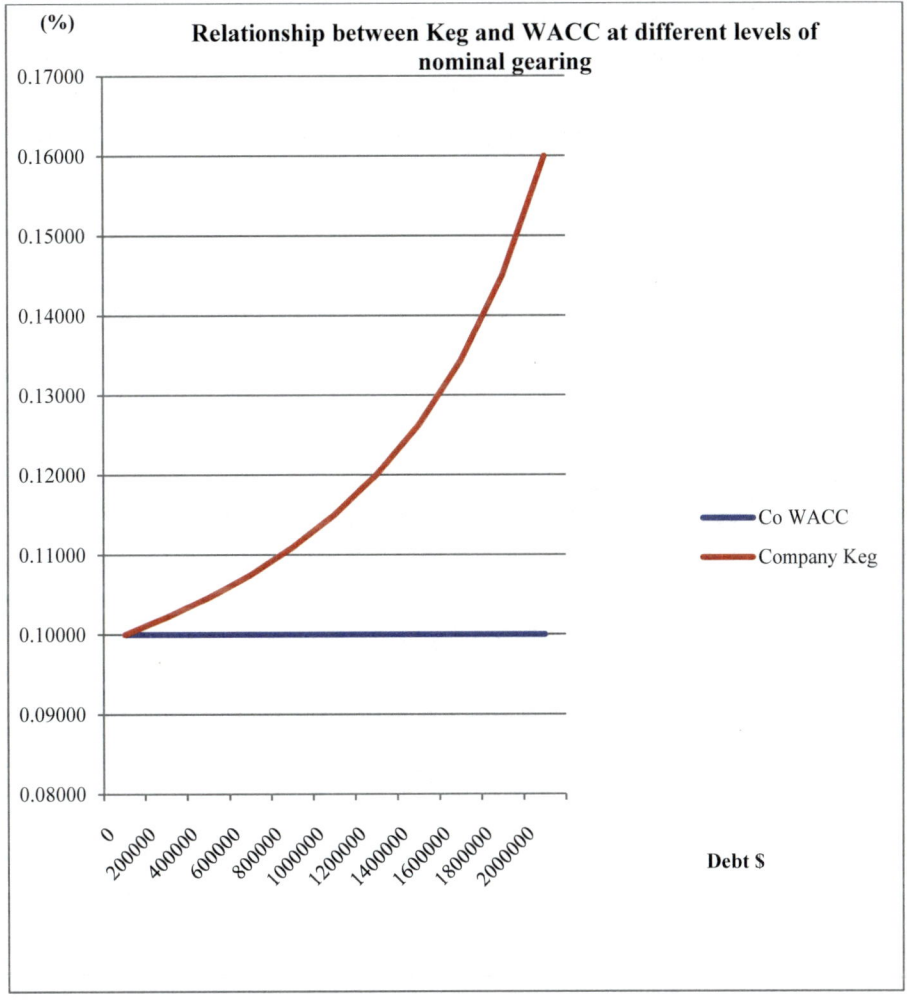

Figure 1: Relationship between Ke_g and WACC (WACC) as the financing combination differs in terms of nominal levels of equity and debt financing

It can be seen from Figure 1 that the WACC (c/PV$_C$) remains constant regardless of the gearing (capital structure) of the company, however measured. However, as the level of monetary, or nominal, debt rises from zero to $2m, the geared cost of capital (Ke$_g$) rises exponentially from 10% to 16%; although as will be seen in Chapter 2, it rises linearly against gearing measured in terms of the ratio of debt to the theoretical market or present value of invested capital. The risk premium on the yield of a share of equity, which rises as gearing increases, is explained in M+M's Proposition 2:

That is, the expected yield of a share of stock is equal to the appropriate capitalisation rate p$_k$ for a pure equity stream in the class, plus a premium related to financial risk equal to the debt-to-equity ratio times the spread between p$_k$ and r. Or equivalently, the market price of any share of stock is given by capitalising its expected return at the continuously variable rate *ij*. (Modigliani and Miller, 1958, p. 271)

Note: P$_k$ = the ungeared cost of equity (Ke$_u$); r = risk-free bond rate (K$_d$); and *ij* is the equity cost of capital (Ke$_g$).

The concept of a 'capital pool' (PV$_C$)

Figure 2 shows how the 'capital pool' or the present value of the company (PV$_C$) and the NPV of equity must remain constant regardless of the financing decision.

The nominal value of equity declines proportionally as it is replaced by each dollar of debt, as determined by the financing decision made.

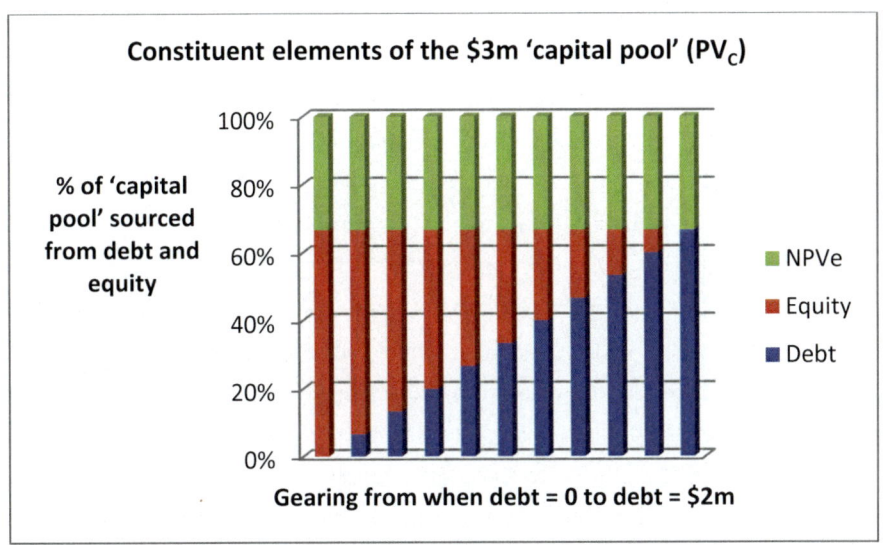

Figure 2: The relationship between the nominal value of debt and equity and the NPV of equity

In this example, with each dollar of debt substituted for each dollar of equity, as determined by the financing decision, the capital pool or PV_C (including nominal debt) remains unchanged at $3m.

This consists of a total of $2m of nominal debt or equity in any combination and the net present value of the equity, which also remains constant at $1m for all levels of gearing, being 33% of the capital pool. The present value of equity at each level of gearing is the nominal value of equity plus the net present value of equity.

Establishing a direct relationship between Ke_U and Ke_g

It is now possible to combine and rearrange Equation (3) with Equation (6) as an equality:

$$\frac{c}{Ke_U} - d = \frac{c - (d \times K_d)}{Ke_g} \qquad (8)$$

The above equality can then be solved for Ke_g by re-arranging to give Equation (9) as follows:

$$Ke_g = \frac{c - (d \times K_d)}{\frac{c}{Ke_U} - d} \qquad (9)$$

where the denominator of the equation *(c/Ke$_U$) - d* equals the intrinsic present value of equity (PV$_e$) as already stated in Equation (3).

Equation (9), shows that for a perpetuity, Ke$_g$ can therefore be calculated when the ungeared cost of capital (Ke$_U$), the perpetual free cash flows and the implicit cost of debt and the value of debt are known. It is also formulated in a way that it can apply equally in a 'world with taxes' because, as will be explained later, taxation is not a variable which affects the rate of return to equity. This means Modigliani and Miller's later correction for taxes with respect to cost of capital was unnecessary. See Chapter 3 for a further explanation.

When the main objective is to calculate a discount factor to assess the present value of equity in a situation where gearing exists or to undertake investment appraisal, using the geared cost of capital is the most appropriate way to do this. When undertaking empirical analysis to value a company and when the beta is calculated through measuring the covariance of the past market to specific company returns, the beta calculated is an equity beta. When this is used in the CAPM, the resulting cost of capital is the geared cost of capital.

However, it is also possible to rearrange Equation (9) to solve for Ke$_u$ as follows:

$$Ke_U = \frac{c \times Ke_g}{(d \times (Ke_g - K_d)) + c} \qquad (10)$$

Equation (10) is a useful formulation in the company valuation process because, to find the intrinsic value of the company, it is preferable to use metrics based on forecasted future cash flows and to discount these using an appropriate discount rate. By using the geared cost of capital derived from the CAPM formula, Equation (10) then provides a direct conversion of the geared cost of capital to the ungeared cost, thereby by-passing the need to ungear the beta and recalculate the ungeared cost of capital indirectly, with all the uncertainties involved. An example of how this can be used is given in the postscript to this book.

Returning to the example; at the financing decision where debt = $1m, using Equation (3), Ke$_g$ can therefore be calculated as follows:

Ke$_g$ = (300,000 - 70,000)/(300,000/0.1) - 1,000,000) = 11.5%

So, for the geared company in the illustration, which has chosen to finance the $2m capital requirement, 50% from debt and 50% from equity, the present value of equity is calculated as follows from Equation (6):

PV$_e$ = c - (d x K$_d$)/Ke$_g$ = (300,000 - 70,000)/0.115 = $2,000,000.

As the nominal value of equity given in the illustration was $1m, the net present value of the company is (2-1) or $1m, all of which is shareholder value added or NPV$_e$ as shown earlier in Figure 2.

Equations (3) and (6), as approaches to valuing equity, were also referred to by Durand (1959) who was an early critic of M+M; as referred to by Miller (1988) in the following passage:

> He (Durand) had proposed, though not proved, as one of what he saw two polar approaches to valuing shares, that investors might ignore the firm's then-existing capital structure and first price the whole firm by capitalising its operating earnings before interest and taxes.
>
> The value of the shares would then be found by subtracting out the value of the bonds. But he rejected this possibility in favour of his other extreme, which he believed to be closer to the ordinary, real-world way of valuing corporate shares, in which investors capitalised the firm's net income after interest and taxes with only a loose, qualitative adjustment for the degree of leverage in the capital structure. (Miller, p. 101)

Durand's preferred way to value a company can be achieved by using Equation 6, using the EV method. According to Miller, both of Durand's 'polar' approaches would give the same result, if applied consistently in a 'world without taxes'. However, there is not a 'loose, qualitative adjustment for the degree of leverage in the capital structure' because Equation 6 shows there is, in fact, a 'tight quantitative adjustment'. Later in the book, it is shown that these 'polar' approaches will give the same result in a 'world with taxes' if the appropriate tax adjustment is made to both equations.

Chapter Summary

- ✓ Capital structure irrelevance was first suggested by Burr Williams (1938)
- ✓ Modigliani and Miller confirmed this in their Propositions 1 and 2 (1958)
- ✓ There are three alternative ways to value a company's equity in a 'world without taxes':
  - o **APV (Myers, 1974)**: discounting cash flows before interest by the ungeared cost of equity and subtracting debt.
  - o **WACC (Miles and Ezzell, 1980(a))**: discounting cash flows before interest by the weighted average cost of capital and subtracting debt.
  - o Equity valuation method: discounting cash flows net of interest by the geared cost of equity.
- ✓ All three of the above approaches yield consistent results where there is no taxation to consider.
- ✓ Modigliani and Miller's Capital Structure Irrelevance Theorem and Proposition 1 can be most simply proved by simplifying an alternative, but equivalent formulation of the WACC equation, which in its simplest form becomes the ungeared cost of equity (Ke_U)
- ✓ The net present value of debt from the shareholders' perspective is zero when the implicit cost of debt is used as the discount factor for the finance costs, further corroborating Modigliani and Miller's Proposition 1 that the value of a company is completely unaffected by the cost or the amount of debt where there are no taxes to consider.
- ✓ The relationship between the APV and 'equity valuation' methods can then be restated in terms of Keg or as Ke_U as in Equations (9) and (10).
- ✓ Because the NPV of debt, as far as the company is concerned, is zero, the relationship between the APV and WACC methods can be simplified

and the WACC element removed, giving the equity valuation method based on the geared cost of capital (Keg).
- ✓ Because the net present value of debt is zero, by implication, changes in the cost of debt or the amount borrowed cannot affect the value of the company as a whole (PVC). This means that 'value invariance' can only be maintained as a result of changes in debt or financing costs if the cost of equity is directly adjusted to compensate for the increased financial risk of such changes.
- ✓ Durand (1959) suggested that the value of a company can be calculated equally validly by either discounting cash flows before interest and tax by the ungeared cost of equity or discounting the net cash flows after interest and tax discounted by the geared cost of equity ('The two polar approaches').

Chapter 2
How the Modigliani and Miller Propositions Explain the Relationship Between Ke$_g$ and Gearing

Propositions 1 and 2 and the relationship between Ke$_g$ and gearing

Returning to Modigliani and Miller (1958, p. 271), part of Proposition 2 was stated as follows:

> the expected yield of a share of stock is equal to the appropriate capitalisation rate p$_k$ for a pure equity stream in the class, plus a premium related to the financial risk equal to the debt-to-equity ratio times the spread between p$_k$ and r.

They derive their own equation (8) as follows:

(8) $ij = p_k + (p_k - r) D_j/S_j$,

where ij = geared cost of equity, p$_k$ = Ungeared cost of equity, r = cost of debt, D$_j$ = value of debt, and S$_j$ = value of shares or equity.

Miller (op. cit.) also referred to the cost of equity capital as having a 'linear increasing relationship' with the debt-to-equity ratio. In their calculation of the gearing ratio, M+M defined equity as the market or 'present value' of equity.

To calculate Ke$_g$ directly from the quote and using M+M's equation (8), it is possible to construct Equation (11), using the notation used throughout this book:

$$Ke_g = Ke_U + (Ke_u - K_d) \times \left(\frac{d}{PVe}\right) \quad (11)$$

In the illustration used in this book, as the implicit cost of debt is 7%, and Ke_U is 10%, Modigliani and Miller's equation would be calculated as follows:

0.1 + ((0.1 - 0.07) x 1,000,000/2,000,000) = giving a Ke_g of 11.5%, which is the same rate as obtained more directly, using Equation (9).

However, as has been shown already, the fundamental or theoretical value of shareholders' equity (PV_e) is calculated separately using Equations (3), (4) or (6), and therefore, from a normative perspective, the above equation would seem to contain a circular argument, because there is a recursive interdependency between Ke_g and PV_e.

Unless Ke_g is calculated as in Equation (9), where there is no such recursive interdependence, PV_e can only otherwise be obtained empirically by observing the listed share price, which can be fundamentally under or overvalued, resulting in a potentially invalid cost of capital being calculated.

The linear relationship between Ke_g and financial gearing based on fundamental values

Ke_g can be plotted against the gearing ratio percentage (d/PV_e) x 100 from when gearing is zero to when it reaches 200%—when the company is entirely debt financed. When this alternative scale is used for the x-axis rather than the nominal monetary debt as used in Figure 1, the linear relationship can be observed. Note that perpetual annual cash flows (c) are $300,000; Ke_u = 10% and K_d = 7%.

The mathematical relationships can be observed in Table 1:

Debt	PV_e	PV_C	Finance costs (f)	Ke_g	Gearing
d	c/Ke_U – d	c/Ke_U	d x K_d	c - f/(c/Ke_U) - d	d/PV_e
$000	$000	$000	$'000	%	%
0	3,000	3,000	0	0.100	0.00
200	2,800	3,000	14	0.102	7.14
400	2,600	3,000	28	0.105	15.38
600	2,400	3,000	42	0.108	25.00
800	2,200	3,000	56	0.111	36.36
1,000	2,000	3,000	70	0.115	50.00
1,200	1,800	3,000	84	0.120	66.67

1,400	1,600	3,000	98	0.126	87.50
1,600	1,400	3,000	112	0.134	114.29
1,800	1,200	3,000	126	0.145	150.00
2,000	1,000	3,000	140	0.160	200.00

The linear relationship is shown in Figure 3:

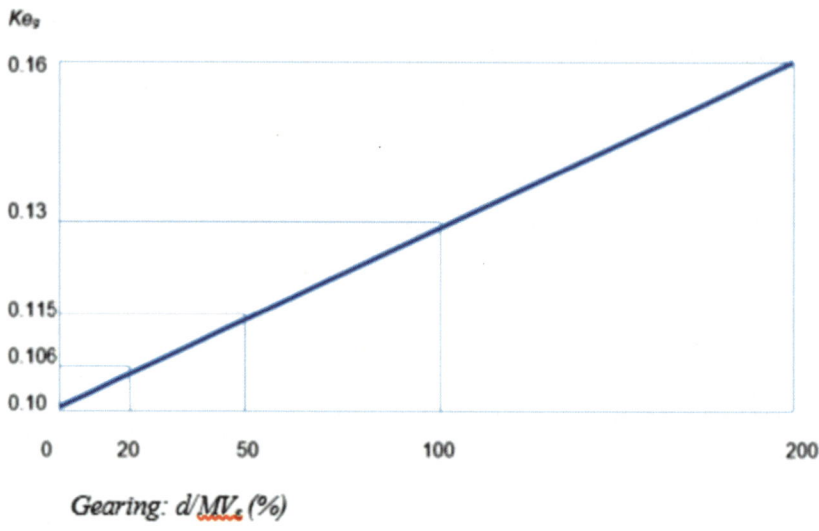

Figure 3: Ke_g plotted against gearing as a percentage of debt to present value of equity

Referring to Equation (11), where there are no taxes, PV_e can be obtained (normatively rather than empirically) by using Equation (3), so Equation (11) can be restated to avoid the circular argument, substituting PV_e with $c/Ke_U - d$ as follows:

$$Ke_g = Ke_U + (Ke_u - K_d) \times \left(\frac{d}{\frac{c}{Ke_U} - d}\right)$$

From the above calculations, this equation yields exactly the same result as Equation (9): 11.5%, therefore the above equation is exactly equivalent to Equation (9) by rearrangement, as follows:

$Ke_g = Ke_u + ((Ke_u - K_d) \times (d/(c/Ke_u - d)))$

Factor out the d from the numerator:
$Ke_u + d \times Ke_u - d \times K_d/((c/Ke_u) - d)$

Combine the Ke_u term with the fraction:
$Ke_u \times (c/Ke_u - d) + d \times Ke_u - d \times K_d/((c/Ke_u) - d)$

Distribute Ke_u in the numerator:
$c - d \times Ke_u + d \times Ke_u - d \times K_d/((c/Ke_u) - d)$

Simplify the numerator by summing $+ d \times Ke_u - d \times Ke_u$:
$Keg = c - (d \times K_d)/((c/Ke_u) - d)$ which is now rearranged, as in Equation (9).

How Propositions 1 and 2 lead to Proposition 3.

Modigliani and Miller (1958, *op. cit.*) also arrived at a third proposition as follows:

If a firm in class k is acting in the best interest of the stockholders at the time of the decision, it will exploit an investment opportunity if and only if the rate of return on the investment, say p*, is as large as or larger than p_k. That is, the cut-off point for investment in the firm will in all cases be p_k and will be completely unaffected by the type of security used to finance the investment. (Modigliani and Miller, 1958, p. 288)

This is the argument that a company should only undertake a new investment if the rate of return obtained from the new investment exceeds the company's existing ungeared cost of capital, regardless of which funds are used or how cheaply the funds for the new investment can be sourced.

The last sentence of their Proposition 3 relating to p_k makes the additional point that regardless of how cheaply funds can be obtained to finance the new investment, the relative cost of those funds has absolutely no impact on the weighted average cost of capital or the value of the company.

M+M states that the Proposition holds because it follows on from their previous two propositions (which are essentially interdependent):

Proposition 1: the market value of any firm is independent of its capital structure and is given by capitalising its expected return at the rate p_k appropriate to its class.

Proposition 2: the expected yield of a share of stock is equal to the appropriate capitalisation rate p_k for a pure equity stream in the class, plus a premium related to financial risk equal to the debt-to-equity ratio times the spread between p_k and r.

However, this book has already explained that this is fundamentally because the NPV of debt, using the implicit cost of that debt to the company, from their perspective, is always zero.

To confirm this, we can take an example where Company A borrows funds at a lower cost of capital than its current ungeared cost of capital (p_k) and where the expected return from the additional investment is also p_k or 10%.

Example:

Company A referred to earlier now has an investment opportunity costing $100,000 which offers a return of 10%. This is the same as their current ungeared cost of capital Ke_U.

Let it be assumed that it can undertake this investment opportunity by borrowing at the low rate of 4% rather than the current 7%. If the company borrows the $100,000 to take advantage of the cheaper debt, will the value of the company increase? Propositions 1, 2 and 3 would suggest that this is not possible in a 'world without taxes'

Using Equation (9), it is possible to calculate the new Ke_g for the whole company (including the additional investment):

Ke_g = c - (d x K_d)/(c/Keu) - d
= 300,000 + 10,000 - (70,000 + 4,000)/(310,000/0.1) - (1,000,000 + 100,000)
= 310,000 - 74,000 /((310,000/0.10) - 1,100,000)
= 236,000/2,000,000 = 0.118%

Therefore, the new value of the company's equity using Equation (6) is:

$$PV_e = (c - (d \times K_d))/K_{eg}$$

= 236,000/0.118 = $2,000,000 which is the same as the existing value, proving that neither the change in amount or cost of debt for the investment of (7–4) 3%, has made any difference to the overall value of equity.

Whilst it is not necessary to do so; but out of interest and to confirm M+M's proposition, we can also calculate the new weighted average cost of capital after undertaking the new investment:

WACC or WACC (post-investment) = WACC = $(d \times K_d) + (PV_e \times K_{eg}/(PV_e + d)$

= (100,000 × 0.04 + (1,000,000 × 0.07) + ((2,000,000 × 0.118)/2,000,000 + 1,000,000 + 100,000 =

= 74,000 + 236,000/3,100,000 = 10%

Therefore, as expected, WACC has not changed as a result of borrowing the additional £100,000 at the lower rate of interest. This is because the K_{eg} of the company has risen to 11.8% as a result of the additional gearing, keeping the WACC at 10% overall, and thereby compensating precisely for the additional risk premium.

Chapter Summary

- ✓ Modigliani and Miller's Proposition 2 states that where there are no taxes to consider, Ke_g increases proportionally with gearing when gearing is measured as debt as a percentage of the market or present value of equity.
- ✓ Modigliani and Miller's equation for calculating the risk premium of gearing and to obtain Ke_g must be adapted and can be rearranged to avoid circularity, by using Equation (9); to ensure that it yields a valid Ke_g in all circumstances.
- ✓ Proposition 3 builds on Propositions 1 and 2 and concludes that regardless of how cheaply a company can source funds in comparison with its existing cost of equity, the value of the company cannot be affected by the relative capital costs. In a 'world without taxes', value is entirely dependent on the comparative rate of return between the existing ungeared cost of capital and the rate of return to be obtained from the new investment.

Chapter 3
Modigliani and Miller and the 'World with Taxes'

M+M admitted in a later correction to their original theorem (Modigliani and Miller, *op. cit.*) that tax savings from additional borrowing do create additional shareholder value, which their original propositions ignored.

Returning to the original investment decision of how to fund the $2m required to set up Company A, it is now possible to re-examine the relationship between company-wide gearing and Ke_g using Equation (9) and including the tax effects.

The following data shows the effect of tax being at the rate of 30% of free cash flows. The table contains data from when the company is 100% equity financed to where it is $2m debt financed, at intervals of $200,000.

Table 2: Relationship between gearing, WACC and Ke$_g$ for the whole company at different combinations of debt and equity originally invested

Nominal equity (e)	Nominal debt (d)	Annual cash flow (c)	Interest at 7% (d x K$_d$) = (f)	Tax at 30%: (c x t$_R$) = (t)	Tax savings (f x t$_R$) = (s)	Net tax = (t - s)	Co WACC or WACC	Company Ke$_g$	PV$_e$ - e = NPV$_e$
$	$	$	$	$	$	$	$	$	$
2000000	0	300000	0	90000	0	90000	0.1	0.1	100000
1800000	200000	300000	14000	90000	4200	85800	0.09917	0.1021	160000
1600000	400000	300000	28000	90000	8400	81600	0.09838	0.1046	220000
1400000	600000	300000	42000	90000	12600	77400	0.09763	0.1075	280000
1200000	800000	300000	56000	90000	16800	73200	0.09692	0.1109	340000
1000000	1000000	300000	70000	90000	21000	69000	0.09625	0.115	400000
800000	1200000	300000	84000	90000	25200	64800	0.09561	0.12	460000
600000	1400000	300000	98000	90000	29400	60600	0.095	0.1263	520000
400000	1600000	300000	112000	90000	33600	56400	0.09442	0.1343	580000
200000	1800000	300000	126000	90000	37800	52200	0.09386	0.145	640000
0	2000000	300000	140000	90000	42000	48000	0.09333	0.16	700000

Table 2 shows that the net present value of equity rises by $60,000 per $200,000 of additional debt substituted for nominal equity or (4,200/0.07) due to the incremental tax savings, but Ke$_g$ still rises from the ungeared level at 10% up to 16% when the company is financed by $2m of debt.

This table therefore shows that Ke$_g$ is completely unaffected by tax considerations and tax therefore will have no effect on Equation (9) as already formulated.

Note also that the present value of equity (PV$_e$) at the point at which debt is $1m = $'000 (1,000 + 400) or $1,400,000, rather than $2m as it was when there were no taxes at the same level of gearing. This is because paying 30% tax on the company's free cash flows immediately reduces the present value of equity by 30% and this applies at all levels of gearing.

In addition, whereas WACC remained constant with gearing in a 'world without taxes', it now decreases at each level of gearing, until it reaches 9.33% when the company is financed by $2m debt.

These relationships are shown graphically in Figure 4:

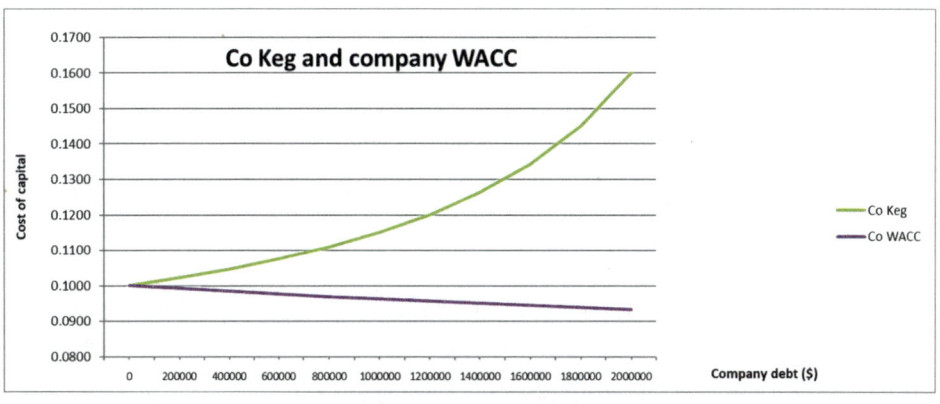

Figure 4: Comparison of Co WACC and Ke$_g$ from when debt is zero to $2m

The graph confirms that tax effects have no impact on Ke$_g$ because Ke$_g$ still rises from 10% to 16% as debt rises from zero to $2m as it did when there was no tax payable. This can be mathematically demonstrated below when tax elements are introduced into equation M+M's equation when nominal gearing is 50%.

This shows that contrary to M+M's later correction to their equation (8), (Equation (11)) there is no need to modify the above formula when taxes are included. This can be explained simply as follows:

$$\text{Because: } Ke_g = \frac{c - (d \times K_d)}{PVe}$$

This can be restated as follows to modify for tax:

$$Ke_g = \frac{c - (d \times K_d) \times (1 - t_R)}{PVe \times (1 - t_R)}$$

But because the (1- t$_R$) modifications must be applied to both the numerator and denominator of the equation, they cancel each other out. This links directly to the following quote:

'... the value of the income is not derived from the value of the capital goods. On the contrary, the value of the capital is derived from the value of the income.' (Fisher, 1930, p 14).

This quote clearly confirms that while tax does affect expectations of future cash flows accruing to equity holders, these changes in expectations in income must also have a corresponding effect on the value of the company's equity.

This shows that whilst taxation certainly affects the present value of shareholder equity, business taxation has no mathematical effect on the yield to equity shareholders, despite the 'correction' made by Modigliani and Miller and therefore the modification they made to their formula (12.c, p.439) seems to have been unnecessary and in fact neither M+M's equation (8) (Equation (11)) or equation (9) need to be tax adjusted in respect of Ke_g in a 'world with taxes'.

By extension, a question mark can put against the traditional formula for WACC:

$$WACC = ((e/v) \times Ke) + ((d/v \times (Kd \times (1 - t_R)))?$$

This equation includes a direct tax adjustment for the cost of debt, which does not calculate WACC correctly, as it assumes that the interest rate applied to the debt proportion of company present value is reduced by the effective tax rate. This is not the case. The presence of tax only affects the available free cash flow to shareholders, through the taxation effects on equity and by implication, the value of equity and gearing. Tax therefore has no effect on either the cost of equity or of debt. The full 7% interest rate remains payable to lenders on the loan and the free cash flow available to shareholders, net of the full interest charge, is then taxed. So rather than tax directly reducing the cost of debt to the company, the cost of debt effectively reduces the cost of tax to the shareholders.

This is a crucial point because including the tax adjustment to the interest rate itself, significantly undervalues the correct WACC, potentially leading to serious miss-valuation problems where taxation is concerned, particularly at higher rates of taxation and in the extreme situation of 100% tax, yields a zero percent WACC, which is theoretically impossible.

To illustrate this, using information from Table 2 above; at the point at which the company has debt of $2m and the present value of equity is $700,000, it can be seen that the available free cash flow to lenders and shareholders comprises interest of $140,000 + the remaining after-tax cash flow available to shareholders (160,000 x 0.7) = $252,000 re-arranged c x (1 - t_R) + (d x K_d x t_R)

WACC is therefore correctly calculated as 252,000/2,700,000 = 9.33%. If WACC had been calculated using the traditional approach, assuming the correct equity valuation was used, it would yield the following in ($'000s):

$$WACC = ((700/2700) \times 0.16) + ((2000/2700) \times (0.07 \times (1 - 0.3)) = 7.778\%.$$

This rate understates the actual WACC by approximately 1.55%. Therefore, using this method as a discount factor to value companies or assess investments, would lead to potentially invalid investment decisions.

Therefore, the theoretically correct WACC formula to apply the effects of tax, is presented below as follows in ($'000s):

$$WACC = \frac{c(1-t_R) + (d \times K_d \times t_R)}{d + e(1-t_R)}$$

$$WACC = \frac{300(1 - 0.3) + (2000 \times 0.07 \times 0.3)}{2000 + 1000(1 - 0.3)}$$

Confirming that the correct WACC = 252/2700 or 9.33%

This equation, based on APV principles, calculates the after-tax cash flows available to shareholders in the ungeared company, plus the annual cash flow savings from the tax shield on interest costs, divided by the value of debt plus the after-tax present value of equity[2].

Company valuation where taxes are involved

---

[2] The WACC equation above can also be presented in its more fundamental APV form, using equation 12 below (without subtracting the debt component), as the denominator:

$$WACC = \frac{c(1-t_R) + (d \times K_d \times t_R)}{\frac{c(1-t_R)}{Ke_U} + (d \times t_R)}$$

Returning to the valuation of Company A, excluding the additional investment referred to above; because company value is affected by tax, it is now necessary to make tax adjustments to the cash flows.

The three valuation equations introduced earlier on can be presented as follows using the component variables:

APV method:

$$PVe = \frac{c(1-t_R)}{Ke_U} + (d \times t_R) - d \qquad (12)$$

Note: Tax savings are represented as $(d \times t_R)$ as a simplification of $(d \times K_d \times t_R)/K_d$ where K_d cancels from the numerator and denominator of the function. This means that the present value of tax savings is completely unaffected by the interest rate and is entirely dependent on the value of outstanding debt multiplied by the prevailing tax rate.

WACC method:

$$PVe = \frac{c(1-t_R) + (d \times K_d \times t_R)}{WACC} - d \qquad (13)$$

Equity method:

$$PVe = \frac{(c - (d \times K_d)) \times (1 - t_R)}{Ke_g} \qquad (14)$$

The APV method (Equation (12)) discounts notional cash flows before interest, but after tax, using the ungeared cost of capital, thereby assuming that a geared company is all equity financed.

In this equation, the present value of the tax savings must be separately added to the formula to arrive at the correct valuation.

The WACC method (Equation (13)) discounts cash flows before interest, but after taxation plus the annual tax savings.

The equity valuation (EV) method (Equation (14)) discounts the net cash flows after interest and taxation net of annual tax savings, by the geared cost of capital.

Therefore, it is now possible to confirm the equality of all three equations, having incorporated all the tax implications.

By using the APV method in Equation (12), the value of the company in the illustration (with taxes) is given as follows, where the relationship is modified to include the tax savings discounted by the cost of debt K_d:

$PV_e = c(1-t_R)/K_{eu} + (d \times t_R) - d$
$= ((300,000 \times 0.7/0.1) + 300,000 - 1,000,000 = \$1,400,000$

This is the same equity valuation as we already calculated earlier in Table 1 when equity was $1m.

Taking Equation (13), the WACC method can be tested. However, an additional step is necessary to calculate this composite rate, shown as follows:

$WACC = (d \times K_d) + (PV_e \times Ke_g)/(PV_e + d)$
$= (1,000,000 \times 0.07) + (1,400,000 \times 0.115)/1,400,000 + 1,000,000 = 9.625\%^*$

*Calculating WACC using the above formula, requires you to already know the present value of equity before you calculate it, which indicates an inherent circularity problem with the formulation, but to verify the valuation, the following formula can be used:

PV_e **(WACC method)** $= ((c \times (1-t_R) + (d \times K_d \times t_R/WACC) - d$
$= ((300,000 \times 0.7 + 21,000)/0.09625) - 1,000,000 = \$1,400,000$

Finally, taking Equation (14), the equality can be verified using the 'equity valuation' or EV method:

PV_e *(EV method)* $= (c - (d \times K_d))(1-t_R)/Ke_g$
$= (300,000 - 70,000) \times 0.7/0.115 = \$1,400,000$

This yields the same valuation as the other two methods.

Note that the WACC method (Equation (13)) with the extra step and circularity involved, is superfluous because obtaining WACC using Equation (13) requires a prior calculation of Ke_g and PV_e.

Note also, that under all three methods, the reduction in the present value of equity compared with the 'world without taxes' $PV_e = (2,000,000 - 1,400,000)/2,000,000 = 30\%$ which is a direct consequence of the effective tax rate (t_R) of 30% being applied to the annual cash flows. This means that whilst tax savings do increase the net present value of equity as gearing increases, the total present value of equity has actually been reduced by 30% at all levels of gearing due to business tax being applied.

Returning now to the equality for PV_e established earlier (Equation (8)), which was formulated as follows:

$$(c/K_{eu}) - d = c - (d \times K_d)/K_{eg}$$

It is evident that the left-hand side of this equality is the most succinct representation of PV_e. With this in mind, the simplest and most direct way to value a company's equity is to apply a tax adjustment to the whole of the left-hand side of this equality, as follows:

$$PVe = \left(\left(\frac{c}{K_{eu}}\right) - d\right) \times (1 - t_R) \qquad (15)$$

This is essentially a restatement and simplification of the APV formula (Equation (12)) and yields the correct PV_e as follows:

$$PVe = ((300{,}000/0.1) - 1{,}000{,}000) \times 0.7 = 1{,}400{,}000$$

This formulation is a far simpler and more direct way to value a company's equity than using any of Equation (12), (13), or (14) and accounts for financial gearing and the overall effect of taxation (including tax savings) without the requirement to calculate the tax savings separately.

The above analysis has shown, however, that all approaches, however formulated, still yield consistent results for an equity valuation with the tax elements incorporated. Moreover, the most intuitive and logical method of presentation, from an equity perspective, is given in Equation (15).

However, for discounting cash flows (DCF) and evaluating the viability of additional capital investments, as a single discount rate, K_{eg} has considerable 'signalling' advantages for investment managers compared to the APV method and over using WACC.

The capital pool (PV$_C$) in a 'world with taxes'

In Figure 2 in Chapter 1, the value of the company, including the alternative combinations of invested equity and debt finance and the net present value of the equity were shown as constituent elements of a 'capital pool', or PV$_C$. In a 'world without taxes', this capital pool remained constant at $3m and the NPV of equity at $1m, regardless of the financing decision.

As explained earlier, when tax is taken into consideration the present value of equity (PV$_e$) is immediately reduced by 30% compared to 'the world without taxes' and the government/taxpayers are effectively appropriated this share of PV$_C$, where the company is all equity financed, but the total 'capital pool' of $3m still remains constant with gearing.

However, whilst the net present value of equity (NPV$_e$) is diminished at all levels of gearing because of tax; it gradually increases as shareholders gain from increased tax savings as gearing rises. As Modigliani and Miller stated in the correction to their original theorem, where taxes are payable, the shareholders benefit from a 'tax shield' with higher gearing and their shareholder value increases for each dollar of debt that is substituted for equity, up to where the financing decision is to finance the whole of the $2m from borrowed funds.

What is of interest 'in a world with taxes', is that the total capital pool (PV$_C$) remains the same as it did without taxes, but is now shared between more stakeholders; equity shareholders, debt holders 'and the government', in differing proportions, depending on the original financing decision made. This is interesting because PV$_C$ or the 'capital pool' for each company liable to business tax now includes an economic measure of the net present value of the company to the government or the company's contribution to national public wealth. In theory, the aggregate present value of taxation from all businesses would be a significant component of national wealth in economic terms.

Referring to Table 2 earlier, at zero gearing the capital pool is shared as follows in Table 3:

Table 3: Constituent elements of the capital pool PV$_C$ (with taxes) when nominal gearing is zero

Capital pool constituents	Share of PV$_C$ ($'000)
Nominal equity	2,000
NPV of equity	100
Debt	0
Present value of taxation	900*
Total	3,000

(300,000 x 0.3)/0.10 = 900,000 and where Ke$_g$ = 10%*

As in 'the world without taxes' when the company is all equity financed, PV$_C$ or the 'total capital pool' is still $3m, now shared by three, not two 'stakeholders'. For every $200,000 of nominal debt substituted for nominal equity, the government's share of the present value of the capital pool is reduced by the tax savings (d x t$_R$) or 200,000 x 0.3 = $60,000 which is effectively transferred to the shareholders.

Therefore, the total 'capital pool' remains constant at $3m as gearing rises, but the relative shares of the government and the equity shareholders change.

Miller (1988) recognised this as demonstrated in the following quote:

> Strictly speaking, of course, there is one sense, albeit a somewhat strained one, which the basic value invariance does go through even with corporate taxes. The Internal Revenue Service can be considered as just another security holder, whose claim is essentially an equity one in the normal course of events (but which can also take on some of the characteristics of secured debt when things go badly and back taxes are owed). Securities, after all, are just ways of partitioning the firm's earnings; the MM propositions assert only that the sum of the values of all the claims is independent of the number and the shapes of the separate partitions. (Miller, p. 111)

Therefore, the total 'capital pool' remains constant at $3m as gearing rises, but the relative shares of the government and the equity shareholders change. It is now possible to calculate the elements of the 'capital pool' when the investment is 100% debt financed. Table 4 shows how the capital pool has changed at this other extreme financing decision:

Table 4: Constituent elements of PV$_C$ or the capital pool (with taxes) when nominal gearing is 100%

Capital pool constituents	Share of PV$_C$ ($'000)
Nominal equity	0
NPV of equity	700
Debt	2000
Present value of taxation	300*
Total	**3,000**

((300,000 – 140,000) x 0.3)/0.16 = 300,000 and where Ke$_g$ = 16%*

In Table 4, it is shown that although nominal equity is now zero, the total present value of equity is $700,000 when the assets of the company are completely debt financed. This means that in a 'world with taxes' the equity holders are (700 - 100) $600,000 better off as a result of the tax savings they have made by borrowing the $2m rather than investing it all themselves, which is the present value of the tax savings generated by borrowing rather than investing the funds, also calculated as (2,000,000 x 0.3).

Figure 5 shows how the capital pool and its constituent elements change as the financing decision moves from all equity to all debt when taxes are considered.

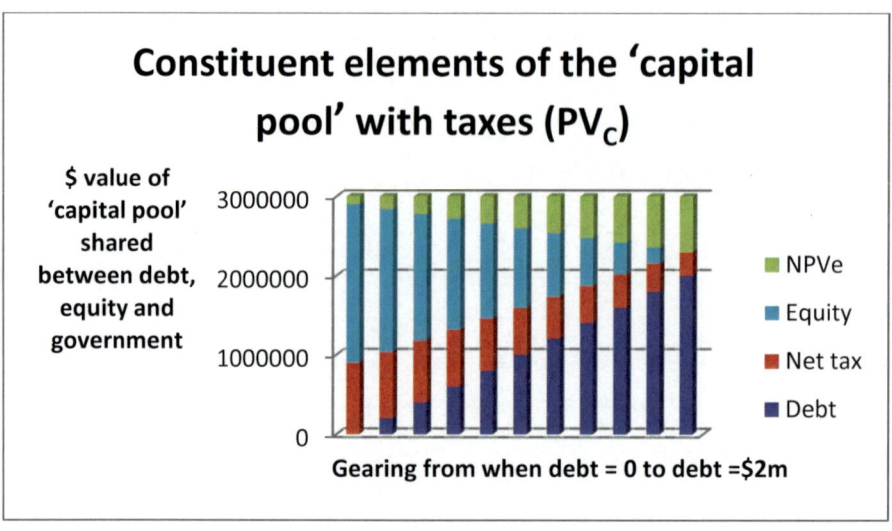

Figure 5: The relationship between the constituent elements of the 'capital pool' as a % of the total present value of the company as debt rises from zero to $2m, in increments of $200,000

The graph in Figure 5 again shows how the total 'capital pool' with taxes remains constant at all levels of gearing (at $3m) just as it did when there were no taxes to consider, confirming that from a wider agency perspective when the government (taxpayer) is assumed to be a stakeholder, value invariance holds even in a 'world with taxes' as the total value of the company at $3m is shared in various proportions between equity shareholders, lenders and the government (or taxpayer).

Immediately tax is payable, when the company is all equity financed, shareholder value of (90,000/0.1) $900,000 is transferred to the government. This loss of value to shareholders is only gradually and partially recovered as the company replaces equity with debt through the financing decision. However, at any particular level of gearing the PV_e is always 30% lower than it would have been otherwise in a 'world without taxes'. In the 'world without taxes', where NPV_e in Figure 2 remained constant (at $1m) at all levels of gearing; in a 'world with taxes' NPV_e now increases from $100,000 to $700,000 as the gearing increases and the government's share of the present value of tax declines from $900,000 to $300,000 as the shareholders increasingly benefit from the 'tax shield'.

Chapter Summary

- Modigliani and Miller recognised in the correction to their value invariance proposition that tax savings do create additional shareholder value as gearing increases. (Modigliani and Miller, 1963)
- In a 'world with taxes', the relationship between nominal gearing and the geared cost of equity (Ke_g) is exactly the same as in the 'world without taxes'
- In a 'world with taxes' WACC declines with higher gearing due to the effect of taxation on the relative values of debt and equity, whereas in a 'world without taxes' it remains constant.
- The traditional WACC formula, which reduces the cost of debt by the prevailing rate of tax, seriously understates WACC, particularly at higher levels of taxation because it incorrectly assumes that tax directly reduces the cost of debt, where in reality, it is the cost of debt which indirectly reduces tax.
- In a 'world with taxes' neither the geared cost of equity (risk to equity holders) nor the cost of debt (return to lenders) is affected by taxation.
- In a 'world with taxes', the present value of equity (PV_e), at any given level of gearing, is reduced by an amount equal to the tax rate applied to the annual cash flows.
- The APV method (Myers, op. cit.) as shown in Equation (12) discounts the cash flows before interest and after tax by the ungeared cost of equity as if the company were 100% equity financed and separately adds the present value of the tax savings.
- The same consistent valuation can also be derived using the correctly structured WACC formula but calculating the weighted average cost of capital to use as the discount rate is an indirect and unnecessary step in the valuation process and involves circularity.

- ✓ The equity valuation method can be modified to incorporate all the tax effects so that the present value of the equity of the company can be calculated more directly by discounting the net cash flows after interest and tax (net of annual tax savings) by one single discount rate, the geared cost of equity (Ke_g)
- ✓ The simplest and most direct way to value a company's equity is to use a restatement and simplification of the APV approach as shown in Equation (15).
- ✓ In a 'world without taxes', the total financial capital pool (PV_C) remains constant, as does the NPV of equity.
- ✓ In a 'world with taxes', the total financial capital pool (PV_C) still remains constant at $3m, but is shared with a new stakeholder (the government or taxpayers) and the relative shares of the financial capital pool attributable to shareholders increases and the government's (or taxpayers') share decreases, as debt rises.
- ✓ The element of the 'financial capital pool' (PV_C) which represents the present value of taxation is an interesting concept, showing the proportion of the value of a company which is available to the government and is effectively a constituent of national public wealth, potentially to be used for future re-distribution or government expenditure.

Chapter 4
Growth Assumptions

The first attempt to formally include a growth factor in the valuation model was published by John Burr Williams (1938). This model was later developed by Gordon and Shapiro (1956) and Gordon (1962), but these models mainly related to the growth of dividends. As already stated, it is assumed that dividends are irrelevant in the valuation process. Therefore, a version of the growth model to be used here will be based on free cash flows available to shareholders incorporating the constant growth component and discounted by the relevant cost of capital.

As already shown in Chapter 1, the WACC is not a relevant metric to use because, when decomposed into its debt and equity components, it can be simplified into the equity valuation model because the debt proportion of the value cancels out and any changes in debt have no effect on the value of a company. The other reason, given in the previous chapter, is that using WACC in its original form creates an inherent circularity problem; in that to value a company using the weighted average cost of capital as a discount factor, requires a valuation of the company before you can calculate the discount factor itself, which introduces a recursive dependency. In view of this, when valuing a company, or its equity, the simplified APV approach or the equity method will be used, neither of which methodologies create a circular argument.

For practical purposes, it is assumed that most successful companies grow over time. Brealey, Myers et al. (2008) state that the valuation of a perpetuity with growth requires the free cash flows to be multiplied by $(1 + g)$ and for the appropriate cost of capital to be multiplied by $(1 - g)$ where g = the constant growth rate.

The forecast growth rate can be estimated from extrapolating past growth rates, where the growth in returns in the past may indicate a similar trend in the future. This can be calculated using the compound periodic growth rate (CPGR) approach based on the following formula:

CPGR = (closing value/opening value)$^{1/n}$ - 1
Where n = the number of periods (in this case years)

Knowing that the annual cash flows (c) are currently $300,000 and establishing that they were $271,719 five years ago, it is possible to calculate the past annual mean growth.

CAGR = ((300,000/271,719)$^{1/5}$ - 1) = 0.02 or 2%

To take growth into account in respect of a perpetuity, where business taxes are payable; Equation (15) can be used to do this if it is modified appropriately for the growth rate.

If it is assumed, from the above calculation of cash flow growth in the previous five years, that the expected growth in the cash flows of the company in the illustration was forecast to continue at 2% into perpetuity, it is possible to build this into the valuation model already derived. Growth affects total cash flows and any anticipated growth in cash flows before interest will also affect the tax proportionally when applied at the same marginal rate of tax, so Equation (15) would be modified for growth as follows:

$$PVe = ((\frac{c \times (1+g)}{Ke_u - g}) - d) \times (1 - t_R) \qquad (16)$$

Where g = constant growth rate
= (306,000/(0.10 - 0.02) - 1,000,000) x 0.7
= ((306,000/0.08) - 1,000,000) x 0.7
= (3,825,000 - 1,000,000) x 0.7
= $1,977,500

As can be seen, using this version of the APV method and building in a 2% growth component into cash flow expectations, would create additional shareholder value of (1,977,500 - 1,400,000) = $577,500 for the equity investors, compared with assuming constant perpetuity of free cash flows.

Now using Equation (14), which is the equity method of valuation; the appropriate geared cost of equity, modified for the growth rate Equation (17), can be formulated:

$$PV_e = \frac{(c \times (1+g) - (d \times K_d)) \times (1 - t_R)}{Ke_g *}$$

(17)

*Ke_g should be adjusted for growth in Equation (18).

However, because the ungeared cost of equity, net of the growth rate must be used as the revised Ke_u, and because of the increased cash flow expectations, due to the constant growth assumption, there will need to be an adjustment to Ke_g as follows, using Equation (9) modified as follows in Equation (18):

$$Ke_g = \frac{c \times (1+g) - (d \times K_d)}{\frac{c \times (1+g)}{Ke_U - g} - d}$$

(18)

= (300,000 x 1.02) – (1,000,000 x 0.07)/((300,000 x 1.02)/0.08) – 1,000,000
= (306,000 - 70,000)/((306,000/0.08) - 1,000,000)
= 236,000/2,825,000
= 8.354%

If the growth-adjusted Ke_g is now used to value the company, based on the perpetual cash flows (including the constant growth component), using Equation (17), the result is as follows:

PV_e = ((306,000 - 70,000) x 0.7)/0.08354
= 236,000 x 0.7/0.08354
= 165,200/0.08354 = $1,977,500

The above calculations show that using the growth-adjusted APV (Equation (16)) or the growth modified equity valuation method (Equation (17)) with the growth-adjusted Ke_g, are both valid approaches for valuing perpetuity with constant growth. Both will always give entirely consistent results if the cash flows are adjusted for growth and the ungeared and geared cost of capital rates are adjusted correspondingly for the constant growth factor.

Both formulations are constructed logically and in accordance with the conventional approaches to incorporating constant growth into a perpetuity and they also account for the fact that the cost of debt can be assumed to remain constant. As can be seen, the APV formula is much easier to calculate because of the way it is constructed.

Calculating the present value of the perpetuity with constant growth is much more complex with the equity valuation method because the geared cost of equity (Ke_g) has to be recalculated based on the constant growth in cash flows and the associated downward adjustment for growth in the base discount factor (Ke_u).

Therefore, in the interests of simplicity, it may be preferable for decision-makers to use the modified APV method (Equation (16)) when appraising or valuing such entities or investments with a constant growth factor included.

Chapter Summary

- Valuing a company using constant perpetuity ignores the fact that most successful companies grow over time.
- Traditional growth models (Williams, 1938) (Gordon and Shapiro, 1956) and (Gordon, 1962) assume constant growth, usually applied to dividends.
- Assuming that dividends are irrelevant (Modigliani and Miller, 1961) a more realistic company valuation model will need to account for growth in free cash flows.
- Whilst it is reasonable to assume that net cash flows before interest might grow constantly if the tax rate stays constant, it cannot be assumed that interest costs or, by implication, tax savings grow constantly. Net finance costs as a proportion of these cash flows would usually remain fairly stable assuming a given level of gearing and stable interest rates.
- Using WACC as a discount factor to value a company, with or without growth is not particularly useful, because to calculate WACC, it is necessary to already know the present value of the company, which introduces circularity into the valuation approach.
- The choice of approach, is either to value the company or proposed investment, using the modified APV method and using the growth adjusted cash flows discounted by the ungeared cost of the capital net of the growth rate; or use the equity valuation method, where cash flows including a constant growth component less interest and tax are discounted by the growth-adjusted geared cost of equity.
- Using either method, the way they are constructed in this chapter, will yield entirely consistent valuations, but the modified APV with growth valuation model is a more direct valuation approach and much simpler to calculate.

✓ The recommended equation to use for constant growth is, therefore, Equation (16):

$$PVe = ((\frac{c \times (1 + g)}{Ke_u - g}) - d) \times (1 - t_R)$$

Chapter 5
The Company-Wide Cost of Capital As a 'Hurdle Rate' for Additional Project or Investment Appraisal

In Chapter 2, Modigliani and Miller's Proposition 3 was introduced. This proposition stated that the 'cut-off point' p_k being the ungeared cost of capital rate (Ke_U) is the target rate that an additional investment must meet to ensure that shareholder value is maintained. In a 'world without taxes', this 'cut-off point' is also the weighted average cost of capital or WACC.

Much of finance theory and practice suggests that the current or company-wide WACC is commonly used as the discount rate to evaluate investments. Several field surveys have established that most large companies use current company-wide WACC rates to evaluate investments (Bierman, 1993; Graham and Harvey, 2001). This widely adopted discount rate is used to reflect that the funds of the company have been sourced from a blend of debt and equity finance. However, in a 'world with taxes' using this company-wide rate may in certain circumstances, erroneously value the opportunity cost facing the owners of the investing company when discounting the cash flows of new investments in isolation.

Shareholder value may therefore be destroyed if a rate lower (or higher) than the project-specific cost of capital is applied to new investments, either as a consequence of unviable investments being wrongly accepted, or economically viable ones being rejected.

Researchers, such as Grinblatt and Titman (2002) and Brealey et al. (*op. cit.*) have argued that the cost of capital of a new investment, acquisition or even an internal capital project may well be different to that of the company as a whole and that using a company-wide rate such as the current WACC to appraise such investments would only be appropriate if the investment opportunity were an exact 'carbon copy' or a microcosm of the investing company as a whole.

There are two main reasons for this in a 'world with taxes':

1. The market risk (or volatility) of returns to the project or acquisition/investment may differ from that facing the investing company as a whole.
2. The blend of equity and debt used to finance the new investment has a marginal impact on the overall financial risk involved and so the company-wide rate needs to take this into account.

As far as the first of these is concerned, Kruger et al. (2011) have measured the betas of acquiring companies and of their targets and found that many companies do not adjust their cost of capital to take account of the difference between the risk profile inherent within the additional investment and that of the company itself. Such companies often overvalue these investments with unfortunate consequences for their own equity holders. They state in the concluding comments to their book:

Using unrelated data on mergers and acquisitions, we also find that the acquirer's stock-price reaction to the announcement of an acquisition is lower when the target has a higher beta than the acquirer. (Kruger et al. p. 29)

This quote sums up their findings in that often companies invest in projects which carry a much higher risk than the acquiring company is itself facing. This may be because of the size or commercial nature of the investment, or the extent to which the risk in the acquired investment is not as well diversified as that of the investing company as a whole.

It is therefore necessary to ensure that the base rate—the ungeared beta, is adjusted for any difference in the commercial or 'market' risk profile of the investment and that of the entity as a whole. Francis and Minchington (2000) highlighted problems of divisional-level capital appraisal and how this is achieved in practice. They refer to Emmanuel et al. (1990) who suggest that the notional cost of equity for each division should be calculated using the CAPM with a beta reflecting the risk attached to the division's activities, but the divisional cost of capital should also reflect the overall funding structure of the group. They also pointed out that few companies did so. Mills et al. (1996) also confirmed this. They found that 71% of companies used a company-wide equity-based beta hurdle rate to value a specific project or division. However, as referred to above, a serious practical problem arises when the beta of the additional investment or division differs from that of the company as a whole unless the cash flows of the incremental investment or division are discounted separately from those of the rest of the company. The problem with differential betas is also a problem when using the APV method. If the betas are the same, discounting the total cash flows of the company and the project using the cash flow adjusted company-wide rate will yield an appropriate total valuation as will be demonstrated below.

It is outside the scope of this book to consider how the specific asset beta for internal investments or for company divisions, which do not involve the acquisition of listed shares, can most appropriately be estimated. In such situations, an empirical analysis of the covariance of returns cannot be measured historically, so how this is achieved in practice will inevitably involve considerable subjectivity and rely heavily on financial and commercial judgement.

Chapter Summary

- ✓ Empirically, many companies use a company-wide discount rate such as current WACC as the rate to value projects or additional investments (Bierman, 1993; Graham and Harvey, 2001).
- ✓ It is inappropriate to use any unadjusted company-wide rate as a discount factor where the gearing and or the market risk or beta of the additional investment differs from that of the company as a whole (Kruger et al. 2011).

Chapter 6
Valuing Additional Projects or Investments

Following from considerations of how companies actually value separate divisions/projects and incremental investments in Chapter 5, this chapter illustrates a normative approach to valuation and establishes whether it is consistent with the method suggested by Emmanuel et al. (*op. cit.*) as long as the beta of the project (division) is the same as that of the company as a whole.

Taking the illustration used and the original data given at the beginning of Chapter 1, and assuming a 'world with taxes' it will now be assumed under these assumptions that the company's directors now face a choice about how to finance an additional investment after they decided to purchase an investment (set up a division) costing $100,000. They decided to source the funds exclusively from externally sourced shareholders' funds. The investment is expected to yield additional annual net cash inflows of $15,000 into perpetuity. It will also be assumed that the ungeared beta of the potential investment, or project, is the same as that of the company as a whole in order to analyse, in isolation, the financing effects on the geared cost of equity capital where the effects of taxation are incorporated.

What are the implications of making the investment in this project for the company's equity holders? There are two ways to assess this. The first is to discount the total cash flows of the company as a whole by the ungeared cost of equity, adjusted WACC or the adjusted Ke_g and the second way is to discount the cash flows of the investment in isolation using ungeared cost of equity, WACC or the Ke_g which applies specifically to the incremental investment.

First of all, the total market value of equity with the additional investment can established by calculating the present value of equity based on the total company cash flows with the incremental project cash flows added to them.

Doing this under the simplified APV method using Equation (15) gives the following result below:

PV_e (APV method) = $((c + c_i/Ke_U) - d) \times (1 - t_R)$
Where: c_i = incremental cash flow; Ke_U = ungeared cost of capital, d = outstanding debt and t_R = tax rate
PV_e (APV method) = $(300,000 + 15,000)/0.1) - (1,000,000) \times 0.7$ = +$1,505,000

Subtracting the previous equity value of the company, before the investment and including the additional equity investment, we now have the NPV of equity (1,505,000 - (1,400,000 + 100,000)) = $5,000, meaning that the additional investment has created $5,000 in shareholder value and would be a viable project to accept. As can be seen, by the additional calculations and steps below, using the modified and simplified APV approach is the most direct way to value the present value of the company.

However, using the equity valuation method at the pre-investment level, where the present value of equity was $1,400,000 and debt, $1,000,000 it has been established that shareholders are currently earning (and expect to earn) at least 11.5% on their funds (after meeting their debt obligations), but the new project, being 100% equity financed will have marginally reduced the overall gearing of the company, so the new company-wide Ke_g or the financial risk-adjusted 'cut-off' rate needs to be recalculated to reflect the new company-wide gearing using Equation (9):

$Ke_{g\,(Co)} = (c + c_i - ((d + d_i) \times K_d)/(c + c_i)/Ke_U - (d + d_i))$
Where c = annual cash flows
c_i = incremental cash flows from investment
d = company-wide debt before the investment
d_i = incremental debt raised to finance the investment
And Ke_U = company-wide cost of capital, inclusive of investment cash flows.
= (315,000 - 70,000)/((315,000/0.1) – (1,000,000)
= (245,000/2,150,000)
= 11.39535%

It is now possible to verify that this valuation is consistent by using the adjusted company-wide discount rate on the total cash flows as in Equation (14):

PV_e (*Equity Valuation method*) = $c + c_i - ((d + d_i) \times K_d) \times (1 - t_R)/Ke_g$

Where Ke_g = company-wide cost of equity capital, inclusive of investment cash flows

= (300,000 + 15,000 - 70,000 - 0) × 0.7/0.11395) = $1,505,000

Subtracting the previous present value of equity, including the new share capital issued of $1,500,000 gives a net present value of (1,505,000 - 1,500,000) $5,000, which is the same as using the APV method.

Whilst it is not necessary, or particularly simple to do so, it is also possible to calculate the value of the company and the investment using the WACC method from Equation (13):

$PV_e = (c + c_i) \times (1-t_R) + (d \times K_d \times t_R)/WACC - d$

But, firstly, it is necessary to carry out the extra step (involving the problematic circularity) to calculate the weighted average cost of capital (WACC) as follows, using the Ke_g as calculated above:

WACC = $((d + d_i) \times K_d) + (e + e_i) \times Ke_g/(d + d_i + e + e_i)$
WACC = (1,000,000 + 0) × 0.07 + (1,400,000 + 105,000) × 0.11395) /(1,000,000 + 0 + 1,400,000 + 105,000)
= (70,000 + 171,500)/2,505,000
= 0.0964

Using this rate, the following PV of equity is confirmed:
$PV_e = (c + c_i) \times (1-t_R) + (d \times K_d \times t_R)/WACC - d$
((300,000 + 15,000) × 0.7 + (1,000,000 × 0.07 × 0.3)/0.0964) – (1,000,000 + 0) = $1,505,000

Subtracting the nominal value of equity gives (1,505,000 - 1,500,000) $5,000 which is again completely consistent with the other two methods. However, calculating the WACC requires the a priori calculation of the Ke_g and the net present value of equity of the company after the investment, also needs to be already known, making it a circular calculation.

Nevertheless, the above demonstrates that all three methods can be used to consistently obtain the correct total company valuation and to establish that additional shareholder value (NPV$_e$) of $5,000 has been created by the additional investment.

However, an alternative method can be used to establish how much shareholder value is created by discounting the additional cash flows of the new investment in isolation.

Referring back to M+M's Proposition 3, the reason for the value creation is the fact that the additional investment yields a rate of return of 15,000/100,000 or 15% which is higher than the 'cut-off point', which in this example is the base Ke$_U$ or 10% equity beta cost of capital of Company A.

Therefore, as the investment is 100% funded from equity and earns (15-10) 5% more than the cut-off point, then the added shareholder value for the investment must be (5% x 100,000) or $5,000.

Can this be confirmed consistently using the three approaches and using the adjusted company-wide cost of capital rates as used empirically by many companies as referred to in Chapter 5?

The APV model in Equation (15) (or Equation (16) if constant growth is assumed) is the most direct way to obtain the net present value of the project and is as follows:

NPV$_i$ (*APV method*) = (c$_i$)/Ke$_U$) - d$_i$) x (1 - t$_R$) - e$_i$
= ((15,000/0.1) - 0) x 0.7) - 100,000 = +$5,000

Note that the correct NPV is obtained because using APV does not require the ungeared discount rate to be adjusted for gearing (unlike Ke$_g$ and WACC) as APV separately discounts the tax savings.

However, using the equity valuation method, if we value the investment in isolation using the company-wide rate calculated earlier, the following is obtained:

NPV$_i$ (*Equity Valuation method*) = ((c$_i$ - (d x K$_d$)(1 - t$_R$)/Ke$_g$) - e$_i$
= ((15,000 - (0 x 0.07) x 0.7/0.11395) - 100,000 = -$7,854

The above shows that at this level of project gearing, using the adjusted company-wide Ke_g to discount the project-specific cash flows would significantly undervalue the project and lead to it being rejected when it would have created additional shareholder value. This method, using the company-wide adjusted cost of equity therefore undervalues the investment by (5,000 + 7,854) $12,854

However, if the company-wide WACC was used, the following valuation would be obtained:

NPV_i (WACC method) = $(c_i \times (1-t_R) + (d_i \times K_d \times t_R)/WACC) - d_i + e_i$
= ((15,000 × 0.7) + (0 × 0.07 × 0.3/0.0964) - 0 + 100,000 = +$8,921 which now overvalues the investment by (8,921 - 5,000) or $3,921

Unlike using the adjusted company-wide Ke_g, using the company-wide WACC results in a significant overvaluation of the project or additional investment. Although, in this case, where the company-wide WACC was used, the investment decision would still have been valid, the above does illustrate that neither approach, using the company-wide discount rates, could be relied upon to yield valid marginal investment decisions, in all circumstances.

This also seems to refute Emmanuel et al's (*op. cit.*) argument that using the company-wide cost of equity, reflecting the beta of the investment and the financial gearing of the company as a whole, gives the most appropriate valuation for the additional investment or division. This would only be valid where the beta of the proposed investment and the company as a whole were the same and when the company-wide geared cost of equity rate was used to discount the total cash flows of the company (including those forecasted for the proposed new investment), rather than the cash flows of the additional investment in isolation.

The above two calculations therefore show the shortcomings of using a company-wide, geared cost of equity rate or company WACC to value the cash flows of standalone investments or divisions, when the financial gearing of the investment or division differs from that of the company as a whole. However, because of the structure of the APV formula, no such problems are encountered with this method.

Using a company-wide rate is only appropriate when discounting the total cash flows of the company (including the additional project or investment) and will only yield valid results when two conditions apply:

1. The beta or market risk of the company and of the project (division) are exactly the same.
2. The adjusted Ke_g or WACC based on the financial gearing of the whole company (including any additional borrowing for new investments or divisions) is used to discount the total cash flows of the company, including the additional project or division cash flows, rather than discounting them separately.

The more direct approach is to use the company-wide Ke_U, using the modified APV formula which overcomes the miss-valuation caused by using the Ke_g or WACC company-wide cost of capital rates. The other approach is to assess the additional shareholder value created by the investment or project by discounting only the cash flows relating specifically to the project, as recommended by Modigliani and Miller in their Proposition 3, by the appropriate discount rate for the investment independently.

This method of valuation can be consistently calculated using any of the three methods discussed in this book, using the appropriate project-specific rate, where applicable. This rate reflects the marginal financing and opportunity cost (and risk) facing the shareholders of the company by investing in this additional project or investment.

To calculate the present value of the additional project or investment in isolation from the wider entity using the equity valuation method,rather than APV, it is first necessary to establish the appropriate Ke_g rate to use for valuing this project or investment. To find this it is necessary to use Equation (9) again, but apply it to the project-specific cash flows:

$Ke_g = c_i - (d \times K_d)/(c_i/Ke_U - d_i)$
$= 15,000 - 0/(15,000/0.1) - 0)$
$= 15,000/150,000 = 10\%$

The equity cost of capital to apply for this project, wholly financed from equity shareholders' funds is 10%, which of course is the same as the cost of ungeared equity because the project is an ungeared investment. Using this rate would, in accordance with M+M, give the same valuation as using the APV method:

NPV_i (*Equity Valuation method*) = $((c_i - (d \times K_d) \times (1 - t_R)/Ke_g) - e_i$
= (15,000-0) x 0.7/0.1) - 100,000 = +$5,000

By implication, the WACC method, using the 10% rate which applies where the investment is all equity financed would also give the same valuation.

Discounting the cash flows associated with the investment by the investment-specific cost of capital is a more direct and reliable approach to appraising the viability of an investment at the margin. This is possible with all three methods and avoids the complexity of discounting the whole company's total cash flows using the gearing adjusted company-wide rates. Using WACC, as discussed earlier is not useful because of the circularity involved in the calculations. Using the simplified APV approach is the simpler and most direct way to assess the financial viability of the project from the shareholders' perspective than using the equity method, as it only relies on using the ungeared cost of capital of the additional project or investment, rather than having to recalculate the geared cost of capital as is required using the equity valuation method. Using only the project-specific rate resolves the indivisibility problem of the project (or division) potentially having a different market risk or equity beta and a different level of financial gearing, to that of the company as a whole, which is the main cause of erroneous valuation when using a company-wide rate.

Continuing the illustration and assuming that rather than choose to finance the additional investment wholly from additional equity, it was decided by the directors that the whole of the $100,000 additional investment would be financed by perpetual debt at the same rate (7%) of interest. Valuing the project or investment, in isolation, using the APV method results in the following valuation:

NPV_i (*APV method*) = $((c_i/Ke_U) - d_i) \times (1 - t_R) - e_i$
= ((15,000/0.1) - 100,000) x 0.7) - 0
= (150,000 - 100,000 x 0.7 = +$35,000

In this alternative and extreme financing situation, the project-specific equity cost of capital must be recalculated by amending relevant variables within Equation (9), as follows:

$$Ke_g = (c_{ic} - (d \times K_{di}/(c_i/Ke_U) - d_i)$$
$$= (15,000 - 7,000/(15,000/0.1) - 100,000)$$
$$= 8,000/(150,000 - 100,000) = 16\%$$

Because the Ke_U of the project is the same as that for the company, the project-specific company-wide Ke_g rate where all the investment capital is borrowed is 16%, which as previously shown in Table 1, equates to the rate for the company as a whole where debt was $2m. The reason for this is that the investment, in this case, is indeed a 'miniature carbon copy' of the company as a whole. The Ke_U, the K_d, the marginal rate of tax and the annual gross cash flows as a percentage of the book value of the total investment are equal, the latter being 15,000/100,000 for the project, compared with 300,000/2,000,000 for the company as a whole, or 15%

As the specific gearing of this project has increased the Ke_g from 10% when the assumption was that the investment was all equity financed, to 16% when it was assumed that all the investment was wholly financed by borrowed funds, the adjusted rate must now be used to discount the additional cash flows from the new investment/project.

This can be also done using the equity valuation method as follows:

$$NPV_i \ (\textit{Equity Valuation method}) = ((c_i - (d_i \times K_d) \times (1 - t_R)/Ke_g) - e_i$$
$$= ((15,000 - 7,000) \times 0.7)/0.16) - 0 = +\$35,000$$

The same result would also be obtained using the WACC method, but as discussed earlier, this method of valuation is not appropriate for reasons given earlier.

All three methods, however, show that compared with financing the whole of the investment from equity funds, financing the investment wholly from debt increases the net present value of the investment (company) by (35,000 - 5,000) $30,000, being wholly explained by the reduction in the present value of taxation being due to the government and this value being transferred to shareholders at 100% gearing, compared to 0% gearing. This is calculated as the change in borrowing multiplied by the prevailing tax rate ($\Delta d \times t_R$): 100,000 x 0.3 = $30,000.

This all confirms that the APV method is a simpler, more direct way than the equity valuation method to establish the viability of the additional investment because it is not necessary to recalculate the cost of capital for the additional investment and the ungeared company-wide rate can be used for the separate investment cash flows, as long as the asset beta for the investment and the company as a whole are the same.

Chapter Summary

- ✓ If the market risk (asset beta) of the additional investment is the same as the market risk of the company as a whole, it is possible to assess the viability of the additional investment by adding the discounted cash flows of the additional investment to those of the company as a whole.
- ✓ Using the equity valuation or the WACC methods, the company-wide cost of capital rates must be adjusted to take into account any change in total financial gearing caused by the additional investment.
- ✓ Using the adjusted company-wide, geared equity cost of capital rate or WACC to discount (in isolation) the additional net cash flows from the investment will not give a valid appraisal of that investment unless the asset beta of the additional project or investment is the same as the company wide asset beta and the overall financial gearing of the company is completely unaffected as a result of the additional investment being made.
- ✓ Using the equity valuation or the WACC methods to validly appraise an additional investment or project, requires the project-specific cost of capital (based on the financial gearing and market risk of the investment) to be used. Using a specific discount rate therefore allows for any potential differences between the financial and market risk of the company as a whole and those of the investment in isolation.
- ✓ Valuing the additional project or investment using the project-specific cost of capital, whether that be using the APV approach, the WACC or the equity valuation method are more direct approaches to calculating the marginal financing and opportunity cost of the additional investment and measuring any additional shareholder value created (or destroyed) as a result of that investment.
- ✓ Using the APV method for appraising the viability of a standalone project or investment is a far simpler and more direct approach to

valuation because where the business risk of the investment is the same as that of the company as a whole, no adjustment to the ungeared cost of capital is necessary to account for any difference between the financial gearing of the additional investment and that of the company.
- ✓ The recommended approach to appraising a company's additional projects, investments or acquisitions is therefore to use the following formula:

$$NPV_i \ (APV \ method) = \left(\frac{C_i}{Ke_{u^*}}\right) - d_i \times (1 - t_R) - e_i$$

*Note Ke_u, should be reassessed for the additional project, investment or acquisition if the market risk (or asset beta) of the new investment is potentially different from that of the company as a whole.

Chapter 7
The Effect of Gearing on the Company-Wide and Project-Specific Costs of Equity Capital (Ke$_g$) and WACC

Using Equation (9) to recalculate the company-wide Ke$_g$, the project-specific Ke$_g$ and the company-wide and project-specific WACC at different levels of project gearing, it is possible to see the effect of financing on all four rates, comparing the company-wide with the project-specific rates. This analysis still assumes that the asset beta, the cost of debt and the marginal rate of tax are the same for the project as that of the company as a whole.

Figure 6 shows the company-wide Ke$_g$ and WACC and the project-specific Ke$_g$ and WACC based on choices of financing decisions from where the project is to be wholly financed from equity to where the whole of the investment cost is to be borrowed—in intervals of $10,000.

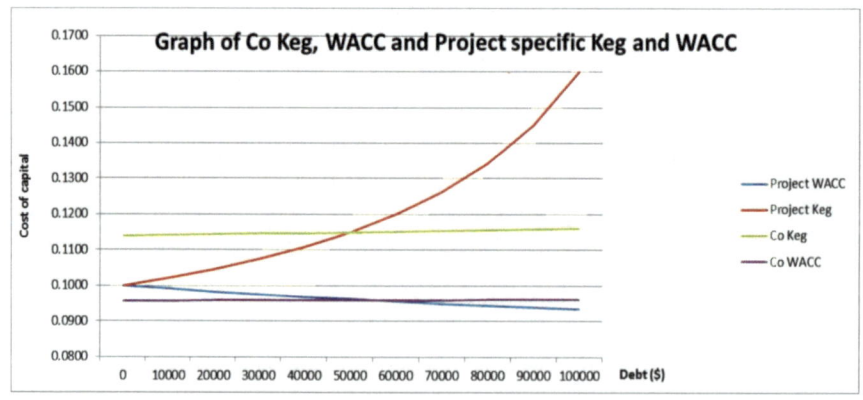

Figure 6: Comparison of company-wide and project-specific Ke$_g$ and WACC for the additional investment project at gearing intervals of $10,000

The relationship between the project-specific Ke_g and the project WACC is identical to that for the whole company at all levels of gearing (without the project) as already shown in Figure 4. Ke_g rises from 10% from where the project is all equity financed to 16% when the company is exclusively debt financed. Similarly, project-specific WACC falls from 10% where gearing is zero to 9.33% when the new investment is exclusively financed from debt. This is because, as stated above, the project in this example is a miniature 'carbon copy' of the company itself (pre-investment). Although this happens to be the case here, following from the point made by Brealey et al. (*op. cit.*) the company-wide Ke_g and WACC rates only coincide with the project-specific Ke_g and WACC rates at the one point where the gearing of the investment equals the gearing of the company as a whole (pre-investment), being, in this case, 50% in nominal terms (where nominal debt is divided by nominal debt plus nominal equity).

From Figure 6, because the asset beta is assumed not to have changed, it can be shown that at all levels of project gearing below the nominal gearing of the company as a whole (50%, in this case) the company-wide Ke_g undervalues the investment, but at project gearing levels above the nominal rate of 50% the company-wide rate overvalues the investment. This applies in the opposite way when comparing the project WACC with the company-wide WACC, where at all levels below the 50% nominal gearing the company-wide WACC will overvalue the investment and at gearing levels above 50% the company-wide rate will undervalue the investment.

This analysis also shows how the incremental company-wide Ke_g rises much less steeply than the project-specific Ke_g. This is because the general company-wide Ke_g is not as sensitive to the gearing of the project as is the specific project Ke_g.

Depending on the expected cash flows of the project and the cost of debt of any funds borrowed to finance the project, the intersection of the company-wide and the project-specific Ke_g will vary, but the key point is that they only coincide at one specific level of gearing. At all other levels of project gearing, using the company-wide WACC and Ke_g rates would be inappropriate for discounting the project's cash flows, unless the total cash flows of the company (including those of the project) are discounted by these rates. Furthermore, if the asset beta of the project and that of the company as a whole differ, it is possible that neither the company-wide WACC or Ke_g rates nor the project-specific WACC and Ke_g rates would coincide at any level of gearing.

Chapter Summary

- ✓ At all levels of project gearing below the overall nominal level of gearing of the company as a whole (50%, in this case) using the company-wide Ke_g to discount net cash flows undervalues the investment, but at project gearing levels above 50% using the company-wide rate overvalues the investment.
- ✓ At all levels of project gearing below the overall nominal level of gearing of the company as a whole (50%, in this case) using the company-wide WACC to discount net cash flows overvalues, the investment, but at project gearing levels above 50% using the company-wide WACC rate undervalues the investment.
- ✓ Because the cost of debt is generally lower than the cost of equity; as gearing rises, project and company WACC rates generally decline due to the taxation effects on the value of equity.
- ✓ Using the company-wide geared cost of equity capital or WACC to discount the project-specific cash flows is only valid when the financial gearing of the project is exactly the same as the financial gearing of the company, without the additional project.

Chapter 8
Valuing Companies When the Additional Investment, Project or Division Has a Different Asset Beta from That of the Company as a Whole

It is now assumed that the asset beta of the project has been estimated at 12% rather than using the 10% rate as previously applied to the company as a whole. If it is also assumed that the project is 100% debt financed, how should the company now be valued?

In practical terms, for additional capital investment projects or investments, which account for a relatively insignificant proportion of the total value of a company, or where they are planning to invest in a similar business area to the one of the wider company, companies would not try and estimate a new beta for such investments. However, when acquiring other divisions or entities or making large corporate acquisitions, particularly in areas which face a significant difference in unsystematic risk profile, it is essential that the managers carry out a full assessment of the beta of the investment in which they are planning to invest, which may well mean that the ungeared cost of equity applied for that particular investment may be different to the existing company-wide rate.

The problem with having a difference between the asset beta of the company as a whole and that of the additional investment is that the total cash flows of the company cannot now be discounted by using a single discount rate under any of the methods under discussion in this book. This is because the difference in beta between the cash flows of the company and that of the additional investment cannot be averaged to take into account the overall financial gearing of the company post-investment.

Figure 7 shows the relationship between the company-wide and project-specific costs of capital when the betas of the company and the project differ:

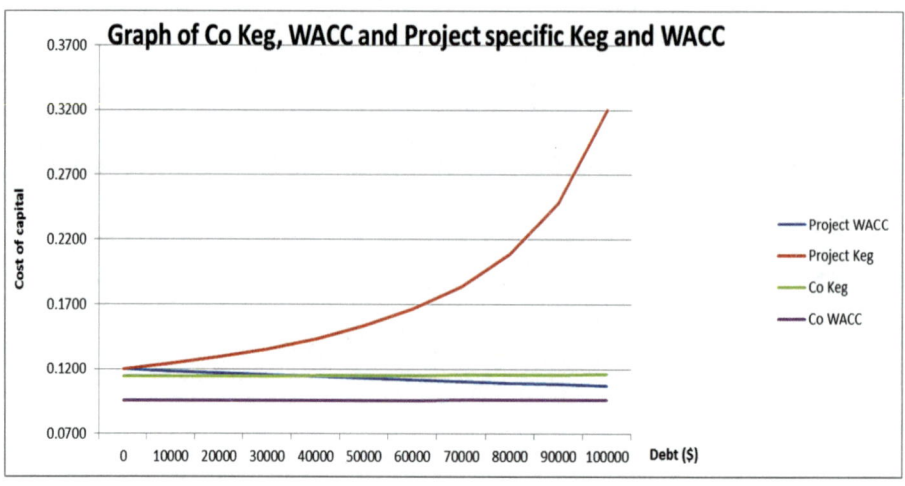

Figure 7: Comparison of company-wide and project-specific Ke_g and WACC for the additional investment project at gearing intervals of \$10,000 when asset beta-based Ke_U for the project is 12%

This shows that an increase in the Project Ke_U from 10% to 12% increases the project Ke_g at all levels of gearing, as would be expected. When the investment decision is to have 100% of the investment financed from borrowed funds, project Ke_g rises to as high as 32%, which is twice the rate calculated when the Ke_U for the project was 10%. In this scenario, the company WACC reduces marginally from 9.64% to 9.61%. The project WACC reduces from 12% (which is the same as the Ke_u of the ungeared project) to 10.72% when the investment is financed wholly from borrowed funds. The difference between the two WACC discount rates at that level of borrowing is (10.72 - 9.61) or just over 1%, which is a significant divergence, meaning that using the company-wide WACC rate to discount the project-specific cash flows would significantly overvalue the investment financed in this way. This divergence is even greater when gearing is lower. If the project is financed exclusively from equity, the difference between the two rates is (12 - 9.64) or 2.36%. More significantly, the disparity between the geared cost of capital for the additional investment and the company-wide geared cost of capital rises to as high as (32 - 11.61) or 20.39% when the project is 100% debt financed. This indicates that using company-wide geared cost of equity rates can seriously overvalue additional investments at higher levels of project gearing. Note also that in the above scenario, the project and the company-wide Ke_g do not coincide at any level of gearing as the two rates already diverge when all of the investment is equity financed.

However, it is possible to evaluate whether shareholder value has been added to the company as a whole by separately discounting the cash flows of the project using the APV or the equity valuation methods to value the cash flows of the investment, and assuming the investment is 100% debt financed.

Calculating the project-specific value using the APV formula gives the following valuation:

NPV_i (*APV method*) = $((c_i/Ke_U) - d_i) \times (1 - t_R) - e_i$
= $(15{,}000/0.12 - 100{,}000) \times 0.7 = +\$17{,}500$

This is a reduction of $17,500 (50%) compared to when the project had an ungeared cost of equity capital of 10%.

As the ungeared cost of equity is 12%, to use the equity valuation method, the geared cost of equity must be recalculated as follows:

$Ke_g = (c_i - (d_i \times K_d)/((c_i/Ke_U) - d_i)$
= $(15{,}000 - 7{,}000)/(15{,}000/0.12) - 100{,}000$
= $8000/25{,}000 = 32\%$ as shown in Figure 7.

Using the project-specific geared cost of equity of 32% when the investment is financed exclusively from borrowed funds to value the project, the following net present value is obtained:

NPV_i (*Equity Valuation Method*) = $((c_i - (d_i \times K_d) \times (1 - t_R)/Ke_g) - e_i$
= $((15{,}000 - 7{,}000 \times 0.7)/0.32) - 0 = +\$17{,}500$

Again, using both methodologies, the resultant NPV of the investment is the same and in the above situation, using a company-wide cost of capital rate to discount the total cash flows of the company and the additional investment, even if it is adjusted for the overall financial gearing, would never yield valid results. This is because the market risk facing the company as a whole and the project in isolation differ and cannot be averaged. Therefore, the simplest, most direct way to value the investment, is the use the modified APV method, using the adjusted ungeared cost of capital, reflecting the higher market risk of the investment.

The next chapter will now consider three additional 'what-if' scenarios to explain the relationships between the company-wide and project-specific rates of return.

Chapter Summary

- ✓ In practical terms, when companies make relatively small or insignificant capital investments in relation to the overall company value, or if the investment is in a business similar to that in which the company already engages, there is normally no need to re-assess the beta value of that investment.
- ✓ When making significant investments, acquiring divisions or making acquisitions, particularly in different business areas, managers should re-assess the asset beta of the potential investment and recalculate the specific ungeared cost of equity associated with that particular investment.
- ✓ When the asset beta or market risk of a division, project or additional investment is higher, the greater the exponential growth in Ke_g with respect to nominal gearing.
- ✓ When the asset beta or the market risk of the investment differs from that of the company as a whole, using a company-wide cost of equity (even adjusted for financial risk) will result in seriously erroneous shareholder valuation and lead to invalid investment appraisal decisions.
- ✓ The simplest and most direct way to value an investment is to use the recalculated ungeared cost of capital, specific to that investment and use the modified APV approach to assess the investment's financial viability.

Chapter 9
Additional 'What-If' Scenarios Relating to the Additional Investment

This chapter will briefly address the impact of the following variables on the relative costs of capital of the project, compared to the company as a whole, using the following scenarios:

a) The marginal rate of tax increases from 30% to 80%.
b) The cost of debt for the project is 4% rather than 7%.
c) The project's annual cash flows are expected to be different from $15,000.

It is assumed that after testing each of the above scenarios all the other variables return to their original levels.

a) What if the marginal rate of tax increases from 30% to 80%?

The effect of an increased rate of tax on the company and the project cash flows is shown in Figure 8:

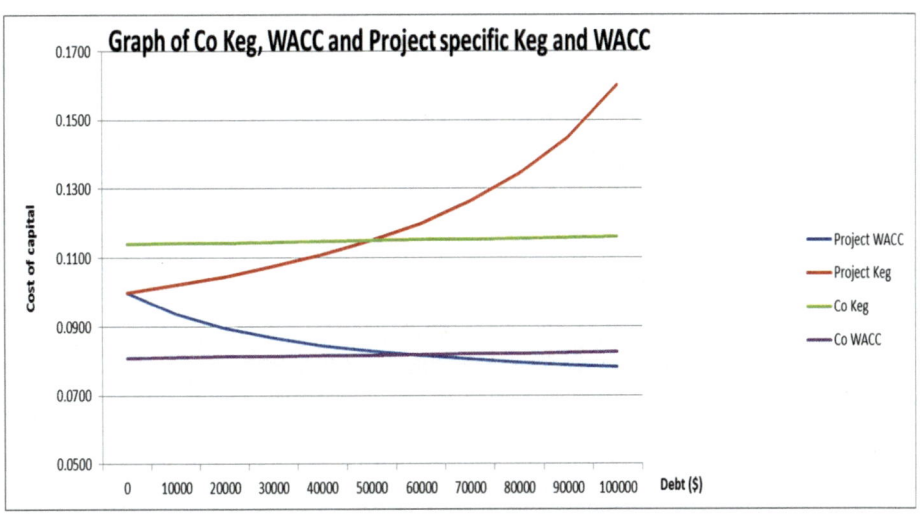

Figure 8: Comparison of company-wide and project-specific Ke$_g$ and WACC for the additional investment project at gearing intervals of $10,000 when the marginal rate of tax is 80%

As already referred to much earlier in the book, this figure shows that such a significant increase in the marginal rate of tax from 30% to 80% has no effect on the project Ke$_g$ because the range is still 10–16%. The reason for this is that the marginal rate of tax is not one of the variables included in Equation (9) to calculate Ke$_g$ and it was demonstrated in Chapter 3 that when Equation (9) was modified to include the tax elements, the taxation adjustments to both parts of the equation cancel themselves out as far as the calculating the rate of return is concerned.

The project Ke$_g$ and the company Ke$_g$ are therefore completely unaffected by taxation effects or by changes in the marginal rate of tax. The present value of equity (PV$_e$) however, at any given level of gearing, is reduced by the increase in the tax rate.

The change in the marginal rate of tax also affects WACC and also increases the disparity between the company-wide WACC and the project-specific rate, due to the tax savings effects on the value of equity and gearing. This implies that the higher the marginal rates of tax, the greater the potential miss-valuation of project cash flows when using an existing company-wide WACC rate to discount the additional investment in isolation.

Note that the project Ke_g and WACC rates still coincide with company-wide Ke_g and WACC rates at 50% nominal gearing in this scenario.

b) 'What if' the cost of debt of the project is reduced from 7% to 4% and how will this affect the cost of capital relationships?

Figure 9 shows the relative capital costs when the project is financed at 4% rather than 7%:

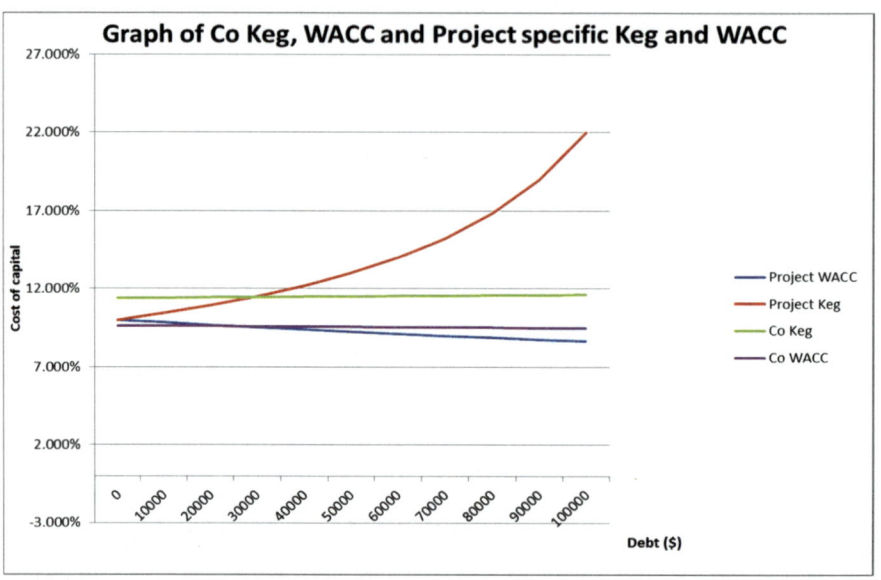

Figure 9: Comparison of company-wide and project-specific Ke_g and WACC for the additional investment project at gearing intervals of $10,000 when the cost of project debt is 4%

In this scenario, the reduced cost of the project debt increases the growth of the project rate of return or the Ke_g as gearing increases. Ke_g now increases from 10% up to 22% at the highest level of gearing above.

Equation (15) formulated earlier shows that for any given level of gearing, the present value of the company is unaffected by any change in the finance costs (d x K_d). The variable (K_d) is not included in that equation, and the present value of the total cash flows on which the valuation of the company is based is independent of the associated finance costs.

This is, as shown earlier, because the net present value of debt from the company's perspective is always zero. This means, ceteris paribus (with or without taxes) at a given level of gearing any change in the cost of debt cannot affect company value, based on the financing decision. Therefore, K_{eg} must always be inversely related to any change in the cost of debt (K_d) to compensate.

In a 'world without taxes', as already discussed, the present value of the company is not affected either by how much is borrowed or at what rate of interest it is borrowed at. In the 'world with taxes', the increased tax savings created by any increase in the cost of debt is counterbalanced by a commensurate increase in the cost of equity, at that same level of gearing, thus maintaining value invariance.

All this means that any change in the cost of debt (at any specific level of gearing) has a neutral effect on company value in 'worlds with or without taxes' and therefore calculating a WACC as a discount factor is not necessary. The determining discount factors in affecting company valuation, therefore, are the ungeared or geared costs of equity.

The above scenario shows, however, the significant impact which changes in interest rates can make to the overall divergence between company-wide K_{eg} and the project-specific rate, particularly at higher levels of nominal gearing.

The project K_{eg} and WACC rates coincide with company-wide K_{eg} and WACC rates at a nominal level of around 30% gearing in this scenario, rather than 50% in scenario a). This is because the lower interest rate for the project increases the relative growth rate of the project K_{eg}, against gearing, compared with the company-wide rate, thus reducing the point of coincidence and affecting the relative rates of WACC as a consequence.

c) What if expectations of annual project cash flows change from $15,000 to $10,000?

In this situation, the movement of the geared cost of capital (K_{eg}) compared to gearing will be calculated when cash flows (c) are expected to be $10,000 rather than $15,000.

The gearing effect of the reduced cash flow expectations will now be demonstrated in Figure 10:

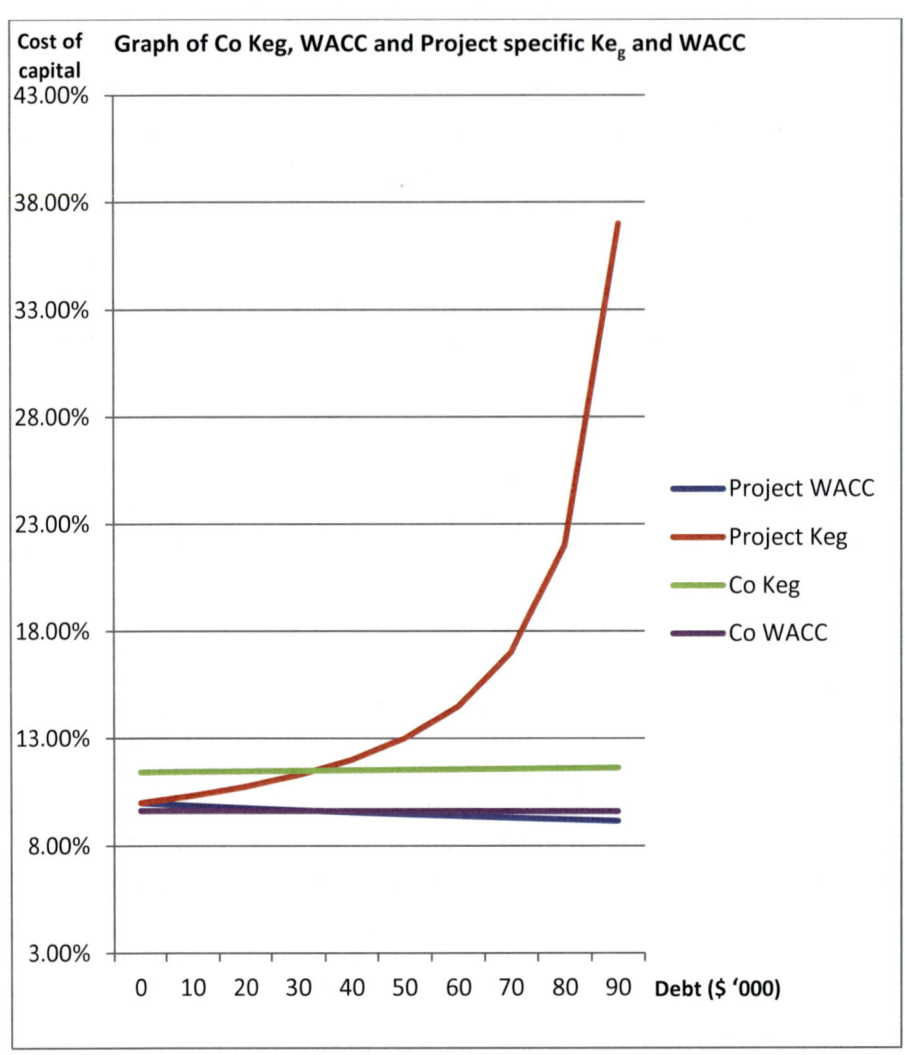

Figure 10: Comparison of company-wide and project-specific Ke_g and WACC for the additional investment project at gearing intervals of $10,000 when expected annual cash flows for the project is $10,000

In this scenario, the reduced level of cash flow expectations clearly signals the increased equity risk of project default, particularly at higher levels of gearing, as the project-specific Ke_g increases from 10% at zero gearing, to 37% at a nominal level of 90% gearing and approaches infinity as the nominal level of gearing tends towards 100%. The reason for the sharp exponential rise is the fact that the numerator of Equation (9) declines as the interest cover of the cash flows diminishes towards the highest levels of nominal gearing. At the same time, the denominator of Equation (9) gets relatively even smaller in relation to the numerator as the NPV of the ungeared cash flows gets closer to the outstanding value of debt. At a specific threshold of nominal gearing, (in this scenario at 100% nominal gearing), the project Ke_g reaches a critical point as the Ke_g approaches infinity and the denominator of Equation (9) approaches zero. Only when NPV reaches zero does the equity valuation method fail to yield a valid Ke_g rate.

To demonstrate this at the 100% gearing level, Ke_g is calculated as follows, using Equation (9):

$Ke_g = (c_i - (d_i \times Kd)/(c_i/Ke_U - d_i)$
$= (10,000 - 7,000)/((10,000/0.1) - 100,000) = 3,000/0$
Which yields a Ke_g of infinity.

At this level of cash flows, the NPV of the investment would be zero, calculated as follows.

NPV_i (*APV method*) $= ((c_i/Ke_U) - d_i) \times (1 - t_R) - e_i$
$= (10,000/0.1 - 100,000) \times (1 - 0.3) - 0 = 0$

When a project is as risky as the one in Scenario c); where the outstanding debt equals the present value of the future cash flows to equity shareholders at maximum gearing; the magnitude of the project Ke_g in comparison with the company-wide rate becomes significantly and exponentially greater to reflect the increased risk faced by the project as it gets closer to yielding a zero NPV. The advantage of the modified APV method offers here is that it correctly calculates the NPV, whereas using the equity valuation method, a valid valuation cannot be determined because the discount rate (Ke_g) is infinity. However, as can be seen later in this chapter and in the next chapter, when NPV becomes negative, the equity valuation method still yields a valid Ke_g and appropriately takes account of the effects of potential 'tax exhaustion', which would occur if the company cannot offset any cash losses against the overall positive cash flows generated by the company as a whole, to reduce the overall tax burden.

The modified APV method, which uses the ungeared cost of equity correctly calculates the NPV as zero, and consistently indicates the viability of the investment by the NPV calculated. In other scenarios, where expectations of free cash flows might be even lower, the equity valuation method and APV will continue to give consistent results even if the project experiences 'tax exhaustion'. Tax exhaustion occurs when cash flows before interest are positive but when the annual cost of debt finance exceeds the annual net cash flow before tax, where $(d \times K_d) > c$) and where the net annual cash flows after interest become negative. In such a situation, the tax shield cannot be fully utilised against the cash flows generated.

Now it is possible to calculate the value of the company and the geared cost of capital (Ke_g) when the cash flows before interest are exactly equal to the interest costs, where annual cashflows from the project are estimated to be $7,000 per year:

Using the modified APV method the net present value of the project is:

NPV_i *(APV method)* $= ((c_i/Ke_U) - d_i) \times (1 - t_R) - e_i$
$= (7,000/0.1 - 100,000) \times (1 - 0.3) - 0 = -\$21,000$

However, if Ke_g is recalculated the following is obtained:
$Ke_g = (c_i - (d_i \times Kd)/(c_i/Ke_U - d_i)$
$= (7,000 - 7,000)/((7,000/0.1) - 100,000) = 0/70,000 = 0\%$

This means it is not possible to calculate the value of the company using the equity valuation method, as using a zero cost of capital as the discount factor will yield an infinite net present value for the project, which is invalid. This shows that in this and in the other special case where NPV = 0, using the geared cost of capital and valuing the company using the equity valuation method would yield invalid results.

In the following example, it assumed that annual cash flow expectations fall to as low as $3,500 and gearing is 100%. The modified APV method would show the following valuation, when excluding the tax adjustment, under the assumption that the perpetual losses incurred by the project cannot be offset against the company's overall positive cash flow by way of tax savings.

NPV_i *(APV method)* $= (c_i/Ke_U) - d_i) \times (1 - t_R) - e_i$
$= (3,500/0.1) - (100,000) \times (1 - 0) + 0$
$= - \$65,000 \times 1 = -\$65,000$

Calculating the value using the equity valuation method requires the recalculation of Ke_g as follows:

$$Ke_g = (c_i - (d_i \times Kd)/(c_i/Ke_U - d_i)$$
$$= 3,500 - 7,000/3,500/0.1 - 100,000$$
$$= -3,500/-65,000$$
$$= 5.385\%$$

Therefore, the net present value of the investment, assuming tax is zero and the losses cannot be offset against the company's wider pool of positive cash flows, yields the following:

$$NPV_i \textit{ (Equity Valuation Method)} = ((c_i - (d_i \times K_d) \times (1 - t_R)/Ke_g) - e_i$$
$$= ((3,500 - 7,000 \times (1 - 0))/0.05385) = -\$65,000$$

However, as we already know from the example used throughout the book, the company as a whole (Company A) has an overall positive perpetual annual cash flow. It must therefore be assumed that the potential cash losses from undertaking this separate investment project could be offset against the overall cash profits of the company as a whole, to reduce its overall tax liability.

The value of the investment can, therefore, be alternatively calculated, using the modified APV approach as follows:

$$NPV_i \textit{ (APV method)} = (c_i/Ke_U) - d_i) \times (1 - t_R) - e_i$$
$$= (3,500/0.1) - (100,000) \times (1 - 0.3) + 0$$
$$= -\$65,000 \times 0.7 = -\$45,500$$

The same valuation exercise can also be carried out using the equity valuation method using the adjusted Ke_g, using Equation (9) as follows (Note that, counterintuitively, because the perpetual net cash flows are negative and the present value of the investment are both negative, this yields a positive rate of return):

Using the adjusted Ke_g, calculated earlier, which as has already been shown in Chapter 3, is unaffected by tax, the NPV of the project can be recalculated:

NPV_i *(Equity Valuation method)* = $(c_i - (d_i \times K_d)) \times (1 - t_R/Ke_g) - e_i$
= (3,500 - 7,000) x (1 - 0.3)/0.05385) - 0
= -$45,500

Showing that using either valuation method yields consistent results, whether tax is included or not.

Finally, this raises some interesting points about the cost of capital or Ke_g in relation to different levels of annual cash flow before interest where gearing is greater than zero:

a. When annual net cash flows before interest, divided by the ungeared cost of capital is greater than the value of debt, or where NPV > 0, the geared cost of capital (Ke_g) is always a positive value.
b. When annual net cash flows before interest, divided by the ungeared cost of capital is exactly equal to the investment, or NPV = 0; Ke_g = infinity*
c. When annual net cash flows before interest are exactly equal to the interest costs or where (c = (d x K_d); Ke_g = 0*
d. When annual cash flows before interest are below b) or where NPV < 0; but greater than c), Ke_g becomes negative*
e. When annual cash flows are less than c), Ke_g becomes an increasingly positive value again*

*When annual cash flows net of interest before interest are in the range between points b) and c), which were between $10,000 and $7,000 in the above case, the geared cost of capital first transitions from being infinitely positive to infinitely negative at $10,000 and then gradually tends upwards towards zero at point c) where cash flows are $7,000. At all levels of cash flow below c) both the annual net cash flows and the net present value of the investment are negative, yielding increasingly positive values for Ke_g as annual cash flows before interest keep falling.

In the special cases of b) and c) above, the equity valuation method would fail to give a valid valuation because Keg would be calculated as infinity or zero respectively. In all other scenarios, whether a tax adjustment is made or not, both methods yield completely consistent and valid results.

The next chapter discusses the extremely rare and unusual situation where annual cash flows before interest are themselves negative.

Chapter Summary

- Changes in the marginal rate of tax have no effect on the company or project-specific Ke_g as the tax rate is not a variable contained in Equation (9).
- Changes in the marginal rate of tax do, however, affect the company-wide and project-specific weighted average cost of capital rates and the disparity between these rates increases with gearing.
- At any given level of gearing, changes in the cost of debt are inversely related to the geared cost of equity (Ke_g)
- At any given level of gearing, changes in the cost of debt have no effect on shareholder value—this is because the net present value of debt is zero, but to compensate for this, the geared cost equity must rise to ensure value invariance.
- Up to a critical point when the NPV of project cash flows tend towards zero, Ke_g rises exponentially and then reaches infinity at that point, where the present value of the investment exactly equals the cost of the investment.
- Where positive expected cash flows are less than the cost of borrowing, yielding negative net present values, the two methods of shareholder valuation continue to yield consistent results, whether or not 'tax exhaustion' is experienced.
- The yield or geared cost of capital mathematically behaves in different ways at varying levels of annual cash flow with respect to gearing as follows:
    a. When annual net cash flows before interest, divided by the ungeared cost of capital, are greater than the value of the investment, or NPV > 0, the geared cost of capital (Ke_g) is always a positive value.

b. When annual net cash flows before interest, divided by the ungeared cost of capital is exactly equal to the investment; or when NPV = 0; Ke_g = infinity
c. When annual net cash flows before interest are exactly equal to the interest costs or where (c = (d x K_d); Ke_g = 0
d. When annual cash flows before interest are below b) or where NPV < 0; but greater than c), Ke_g becomes negative.
e. When annual cash flows are less than c), Ke_g becomes an increasingly positive value again.

Chapter 10
Negative Cash Flows

When forecast annual cash flows before interest themselves are negative and it is assumed that these losses cannot be offset against other cash profits of the company as a whole, the present value of the additional investment will be completely unaffected by different combinations of debt and equity, or financial gearing, as in the 'world without taxes'. Therefore, where there are negative cash flows, the value invariance of Modigliani and Miller's Proposition 1 at different levels of gearing will still hold, as would apply to viable investments, not subject to income tax. Negative cash flows destroy shareholder value directly. In other words, when negative cash flows are forecast, shareholders are not only risking their original equity investment but investing in a project may require them to contribute further capital from their private investments or borrow to fund these additional losses. For this reason, a rational investor would not invest in a company or project where cash flows are forecast to be negative into perpetuity. However, it is of interest to test the validity of the APV and equity valuation approaches and their consistency with each other under these special (albeit unrealistic) circumstances.

This can be determined by assuming that the forecast cash flows for the additional investment are ($3,500) rather than +$3,500, where gearing is still 100%, the ungeared cost of equity is 10%, and all the $100,000 is invested by the shareholders.

Because there is an overall cash loss, to demonstrate value invariance in the case of negative cash flows, unlike in the previous chapter, it will be assumed that the losses incurred by the additional investment, in this case, cannot be offset against the positive cash flows of the company as a whole.

Therefore, the tax rate in this situation is assumed to be zero, based on the fact that the negative cash flows into perpetuity mean that no tax would be payable and perpetual negative cash flows cannot, by definition, allow the offset of losses against any future taxable cash flows in a standalone investment.

The present value of the project would therefore be as follows, using the modified APV method:

NPV_i *(APV method)* $= ((c_i/Ke_U) - d_i) \times (1 - t_R) - e$
$= (-3,500/0.1) \times (1 - 0^*) - 100,000$
$= -35,000/0.1 - 100,000 = -\$135,000$

*Note that the effective rate of tax with negative cash flows, in this special case, is assumed to be zero.

This shows that the shareholders have invested their $100,000 and would need to contribute or borrow a further $35,000 to fund these anticipated losses.

Now the same valuation can be undertaken using the equity valuation method and the adjusted Ke_g, using Equation (9) would be as follows:

$Ke_g = c_i - (d_i \times K_d/(c_i/Ke_U - d_i)$
$= -3,500 /(-3,500/0.1)$
$= (-3,500/-35,000)$
$= -3,500/-35,000 = 10\%$

The valuation under the equity valuation method, with no tax adjustment included, is as follows:

NPV_i *(Equity Valuation method)* $= (c_i - (d_i \times K_d)/Ke_g) - e_i$
$= ((-3,500)/0.1) - 100,000$
$= -\$135,000$

If it now assumed that instead of investing the $100,000 themselves, it was decided to borrow all of the $100,000, it is possible to calculate the NPV of the investment under this scenario:

NPV_i *(APV method)* $= ((c_i/Ke_U) - d_i) \times (1 - t_R) - e$
$= ((-3,500/0.1) - 100,000) \times (1 - 0^*) - 0$
$= -35,000 - 100,000 = -\$135,000$

This gives the same valuation as when the new investment was all financed from additional shareholders' funds.

To check the valuation using the equity valuation method it is first necessary to re-calculate the geared cost of capital:

Keg = c_i - (d_i x K_d/(c_i/Ke_U - d_i))
= -3,500 – (100,000 x 0.07) /(-3,500/0.1 – 100,000)
= (-10,500/-135,000) = 7.777%

The valuation under the equity valuation method, with no tax adjustment, is as follows:

NPV_i *(Equity Valuation method)* = (c_i - (d_i x K_d)/Ke_g) - e_i
= ((-3,500 – (100,000 x 0.07)/0.0777) - 0)
= -$135,000

Therefore, under both methods of valuation and however financed, a consistent valuation of the company is still observed when negative cash flows are forecast into perpetuity. This shows that when negative cash flows are forecast, where it is assumed that no taxes are payable and cash losses cannot be offset against a wider pool of cash profits, the value of the company, or in this case the additional investment, remains unaffected by gearing. In addition, when forecast cash flows are negative, the relationship between the geared cost of equity and WACC differs with respect to gearing, compared to when forecast cash flows are positive and this is illustrated in Figure 11:

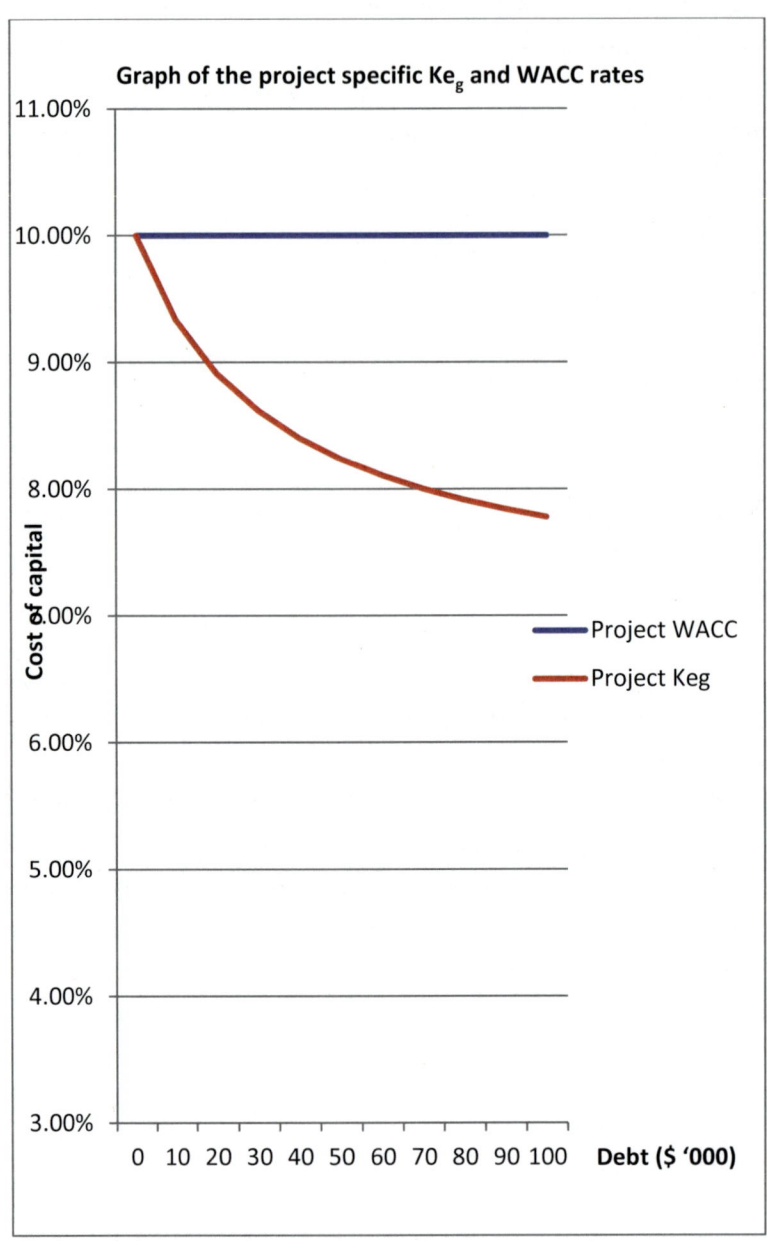

Figure 11: Relationship between the project-specific WACC and geared cost of equity in the situation where forecast project cash flows are -$3,500:

It can be seen from Figure 11, that unlike when cash flows are positive, the project-geared cost of capital (Ke$_g$) decreases with gearing. At zero gearing, the geared cost of equity is 10% and at 100% gearing the geared cost of equity is 7.77%. Although WACC was not calculated for the scenario with negative cash flows, for reasons given earlier in the book; had WACC been calculated at all levels of project gearing, it would be seen that the project WACC would remain constant at 10% as per Modigliani and Miller's Proposition 1 (assuming no taxes are payable with negative cash flows).

However, in the case of Company A, the company as a whole was projected to generate $300,000 per annum, before the additional investment was considered.

In reality therefore, the $3,500 cash loss on the additional investment could be offset against the total positive cash flows of the company, reducing the net cash flow of the company as a whole by $3,500. The implications of this are that the tax liability of the company would be reduced by this loss, calculated as follows:

Assuming the $100,000 was all invested by shareholders, as the cash loss could be offset against the wider company's positive cash flows, 30% of the present value of these cash losses could avoided through tax savings, so the value of the company using the modified APV method would be as follows:

NPV$_i$ (*APV method*) = $((c_i/Ke_U) - d_i) \times (1 - t_R) - e$
= $((-3,500/0.1 - 0) \times (1 - 0.3) - 100,000$
= $-24,500 - 100,000 = -\$124,500$

To check the valuation using the equity valuation method it is first necessary to re-calculate the geared cost of capital:

Keg = $(c_i - (d_i \times K_d)/(c_i/Ke_U - d_i)$
= $-3,500 - (0 \times 0.07)/(-3,500/0.1 - 0)$
= $(-3,500/-35,000) = 10\%$

The valuation under the equity valuation method, is as follows:

NPV$_i$ (*Equity Valuation method*) = $(c_i - (d_i \times K_d) \times (1 - t_R)/Ke_g) - e_i$
= $((-3,500 - (0 \times 0.07) \times 0.7)/0.1) - 100,000$
= $-\$124,500$

If it is now assumed that all the $100,000 was borrowed, the effect on valuation would be as follows:

NPV_i *(APV method)* $= ((c_i/Ke_U) - d_i) \times (1 - t_R) - e$
$= ((-3,500/0.10 - 100,000) \times (1 - 0.3*) - 0$
$= (-35,000 - 100,000) \times 0.7 = -\$94,500$

To check the valuation using the equity valuation method it is first necessary to recalculate the geared cost of capital:

$Keg = (c_i - (d_i \times K_d)/(c_i/Ke_U - d_i)$
$= -3,500 - (100,000 \times 0.07)/(-3,500/0.1 - 100,000)$
$= (-10,500/-135,000) = 7.777\%$

The valuation under the equity valuation method, is as follows:

NPV_i *(Equity Valuation method)* $= (c_i - (d_i \times K_d) \times (1 - t_R)/Ke_g) - e_i$
$= ((-3,500 - (100,000 \times 0.07) \times 0.7/0.0777) - 0)$
$= -\$94,500$

So again, the adjusted APV and the equity valuation methods yield consistent results. It also shows that when it is assumed that the cash losses for the investment can be offset against the wider pool of positive cash flows of Company A as a whole, a tax saving can be made. In addition, the change in gearing between the two extreme forms of financing the investment yield different valuations, assuming the interest payable on the borrowing can be offset against the tax liability of the wider company. Financing the investment wholly through borrowing as compared to wholly through shareholders' funds yields a positive increase in present value of $(d \times t_R)$ or $100,000 \times 30\% = \$30,000$.

Chapter Summary

✓ If negative cash flows are forecast and these losses cannot be offset against a wider pool of cash profits, changes in capital structure (financial gearing) will have no effect on the shareholder value of the company as in the 'world without taxes'—meaning that in these circumstances Modigliani and Miller's Proposition 1 still applies, because no taxes are payable in this unusual situation.
✓ If negative cash flows are forecast; the APV and the equity valuation method continue to yield consistent results.
✓ The relationship between Ke_g and gearing differs when forecast cash flows are negative. In such situations, Ke_g undergoes an exponential decay, falling from the 'base' Ke_U rate at zero gearing and then declining more and more gradually as nominal gearing rises to 100%
✓ WACC remains constant at all levels of gearing where negative cash flows are forecast because in this situation it has been assumed that no taxes are payable and therefore WACC remains equal to Ke_u as per Modigliani and Miller's Proposition 1.
✓ In reality, however, projected cash losses of a potential investment and any interest payable on borrowings to finance such investments, can be offset against a wider pool of positive cash flows of a profitable company overall, meaning that destruction of shareholder value is reduced by the resulting tax savings.

Chapter 11
Implications of the Above Analysis for Valuing Companies and Investment Projects

When valuing additional projects or making incremental investments based on financing decisions involving different levels of gearing, the APV method, the equity valuation method, and the WACC methods are all entirely consistent in the valuations yielded, even when taking into account all the effects of corporate taxes.

The most relevant discount factor to use in valuing a company is the geared cost of equity, calculated in an alternative way to Modigliani and Miller's equation (8) in their 1958 paper, which avoids the circularity issue inherent in that equation. However, after some manipulation and simplifications of the various valuation formulae, it has been demonstrated in this book that the simplest and most direct method to value a company is to use a modified form of the APV formula, whether to value the company as a whole or to value additional projects, investments or potential acquisitions.

This valuation approach is preferred, not only because of its simplicity but also because there is a view that the inappropriate use of a company-wide WACC underestimates the economic cost of capital which has been addressed by several contributors, including Rutterford (2000) suggested from empirical evidence that the undervaluation approaches 1% and concludes that managers add a premium to the discount rate used to appraise many projects and investments to compensate for this. As already cited above, other researchers have also confirmed Rutterford's findings about the use of inappropriate cost of capital rates. The analysis undertaken in this book demonstrates how these findings would be expected based given the widespread use of the traditional WACC equation which adjusts K_d directly by the rate of taxation and based on how these rates diverge at various levels of gearing and as affected by other variables, such as the expected cash flows, the tax and interest rates and the betas of the company and separate projects or investments respectively.

It is interesting that some contributors have proposed that there is a case for WACC to be upwardly adjusted for the additional risks of 'tax exhaustion' and the possibility of default and associated bankruptcy costs (Miles and Ezzell, 1985; Koziol, 2014) to compensate for such overvaluations.

From the analysis undertaken in this book, it may be possible to explain this overvaluation phenomenon as being mainly due to the systematic use of the inappropriate cost of capital rates and applying the company-wide rates, rather than the project-specific rates to discount incremental cash flows, when either the financial gearing of the project differs from that of the company as a whole, or more significantly, where the market risks or asset betas of such projects are much higher than the current or company-wide rate. These, rather than other factors, such as ignoring bankruptcy costs, better explain such findings from a mathematical perspective.

Using the project-specific APV or the equity valuation method, adjusted for any difference in the asset beta to discount project net cash flows, as recommended in this book, would therefore act as a reasonable proxy for this additional risk premium, even when a constant growth in the perpetuity is assumed.

Doing so may help to avoid unnecessary complexity in the process of company valuation, in what is already a fairly complex and uncertain exercise.

Chapter Summary

- All three methods of investment appraisal considered in this book (APV, equity valuation and WACC) yield entirely consistent results in most situations.
- Using company-wide cost of capital rates, adjusted for the overall financial gearing of the company, are only valid if the beta or market risk of the project or investment is the same as that for the company as a whole and only then when the total cash flows of the company, including those relating to the additional project or investment are discounted using these rates.
- Empirical evidence would suggest that using a company-wide WACC specifically, leads to the systematic overvaluation of such projects or investments and these findings are supported through the mathematical analysis in the preceding chapters. In addition, most significantly, at higher levels of gearing, using a company-wide WACC or Ke_g will tend to significantly incorrectly value such investments, particularly if the traditional method of calculating WACC is used.
- It is simpler, and more appropriate, to use project or investment-specific cost of capital rates to independently discount the cash flows of such projects or investments to arrive at the appropriate shareholder value of the investment.
- The modified APV method has a particular advantage over the equity valuation method, or using WACC, as it uses the base discount equity rate of the ungeared company or that of the investment project where that differs, and yields a valid net present value for such investments or for the value of the company as a whole, in all circumstances, in a simple and direct way.

Chapter 12
Conclusions

From a company's perspective, the NPV of any debt instrument is zero. This is why changes in the capital structure through the addition of debt or variations in the implicit interest rates or other terms of the loan instruments cannot affect the value of a company as a whole, where there are no taxes to consider. The fact that the WACC formula expressed in an alternative form can be simplified as the ungeared cost of equity effectively provides a simple proof for the *Law of the Conservation of Investment Value* of John Burr Williams and the *Capital Structure Irrelevance Theorem* of Modigliani and Miller.

Because of this, the economic (cash-based) valuation model for a company can be simplified and the WACC formula, although entirely consistent with APV and EV in its output, becomes irrelevant in the valuation process, through circularity of argument and because it can be restated more simply as the EV formula (Equation (6)) formulated in chapter 1, or even more simply as the modified APV formula (Equation (15)) formulated in chapter 3.

In a 'world without taxes', it is possible to construct an alternative, more direct mathematical relationship between the asset beta-based ungeared cost of equity (Ke_U) and the equity beta-based geared cost of equity (Ke_g), as shown in Equation (10).

It has also been demonstrated that the fundamental relationship in Equation (9) still holds when tax elements and a constant growth factor are included, which means that there is no need to modify this equation for equity stock yield as M+M concluded was required for their equation (8) in their 'Correction for Taxation' in their equation (12.c) (*op. cit.*) By extension, the validity of the modified WACC formula with the direct tax adjustment to the cost of debt can also be questioned and it can therefore be concluded that neither the cost of equity or the cost of debt are themselves affected by the presence or absence of taxation.

By returning to the fundamentals of corporate valuation, if the appropriate discount rates are used, it is possible to reconcile all three alternatively presented equity valuation models discussed in this book; the adjusted present value (APV), the WACC and the 'equity valuation' methods and consistency in valuation still applies when all taxation effects have been taken account of and even when cash flows are negative.

Throughout the book, it is clearly demonstrated that because the net present value of debt from the company's perspective, in the absence of tax, is always zero, using the implicit cost of that debt, the WACC valuation method becomes a superfluous metric, also involving a problematic circularity of argument. Therefore, the only two fundamental methods of valuation which are necessary for company or project evaluation are the APV formula in its unmodified or modified forms or the equity valuation formula. Using the equity valuation method gives a clearer signal of the level of equity risk inherent in the investment, at any specific level of gearing by using the appropriate geared cost of equity as the relevant discount factor, but can be seen to give invalid results at some critical points, where NPV is zero or where Ke_g itself is zero. However, it is clear that using the modified APV approach is a much simpler and more direct method to value companies, separate capital investments or potential acquisitions, particularly if constant growth is assumed.

When constant growth is taken into account. The simplified adjusted present value and equity valuation methods both yield entirely consistent results, although they are constructed quite differently. Using the EV method requires the geared cost of capital to be recalculated and adjusted for growth, using a modified form to determine the correct present value.

A further point raised in this book concerns the valuation of new projects or investments. The book confirms that the APV method, the equity valuation and the WACC methods if used appropriately, all provide entirely consistent results when valuing individual companies and projects (including taxes), as long as the appropriate discount rates, whether they are company-wide or project-specific are used in the right circumstances. The modified APV formula also gives the correct valuation for an additional project or investment, using the company-wide ungeared cost of capital when the gearing of the additional investment differs from the overall gearing of the company. However, using WACC or the equity valuation method in such circumstances, using the company-wide rates, both yield incorrect valuations.

Where asset betas differ between the company as a whole and the additional investment or project, company-wide rates are never appropriate for discounting the total cash flows of the company or for discounting the cash flows of the project in isolation. In such circumstances, only the project-specific cost of capital rate should be used to discount the project-specific net cash flows, reflecting the different risk profile of the additional investment. By implication, the widespread use of company-wide geared cost of equity or WACC for project-specific investment appraisal should be abandoned in the interests of correctly assessing and appraising shareholder value.

When projected cash flows are negative, and unless these losses or the interest on borrowing can be offset against a wider pool of positive cash flows, Modigliani and Miller's Proposition 1 (as in the 'world without taxes') holds and the (negative) present value of the equity investment is unaffected by the gearing of the company, and WACC remains constant at all levels of gearing.

Finally, it is concluded that the equity valuation method is a useful metric as it is based on a single risk-adjusted 'hurdle rate' (using Equation 9) for the appraisal and evaluation of equity investments that represents the real economic cost of capital facing the owners of the company. However, the modified APV method yields completely valid and consistent valuation results in all circumstances, including where constant growth assumptions or negative cash flows apply, and is much simpler to use in such analyses.

Bibliography

Bierman, H. J. (1993) 'Capital budgeting in 1992: a survey', *Financial Management*, **22**, 24.

Brealey, R., Myers, S. and Allen, F. (2008) *Principles of Corporate Finance*, New York, NY: McGraw-Hill.

Durand, D. (1959) 'The cost of capital, corporation finance and the theory of investment: Comment', *American Economic Review*, **49**, 4, 639–55

Emmanuel, C. R., Otley, D. and Merchant, K. (1990) *Accounting for Management Control*, London: Chapman & Hall.

Fama, E. (1974) 'The empirical relationship between the dividend and investment decisions of firms', *American Economic Review*, **64**, 304–18.

Fisher, I (1930), 'The Theory of Interest: As Determined by Impatience to Spend Income and Opportunity to Invest it', New York, Macmillan.

Francis, G. and Minchington, C. (2000) 'Value Based Metrics as Divisional Performance Measures', *Value Based Management*, Arnold G., Davies M. (Eds.).

Graham, J. R. and Campbell, R. H. (2001) 'The theory and practice of corporate finance: evidence from the field', *Journal of Financial Economics*, **60**, 187–243.

Grinblatt, M. and Titman, S. (2002) *Financial Markets and Corporate Strategy*, New York, NY: McGraw-Hill.

Koziol, C. (2014) 'A simple correction of the WACC discount rate for default risk and bankruptcy costs', *Review of Quantitative Finance and Accounting*, **42**, 4, 653–66.

Kruger et al. (2011) 'The WACC fallacy: the real effects of using a unique discount rate', Geneva Finance Research Institute, University of Geneva.

Markowitz, H. (1952) 'Portfolio selection', *Journal of Finance*, **7**, 77–91. https://doi.org/10.1111/j.1540–6261.1952.tb01525.x.

Miles, J. A. and Ezzell, J. R. (1980) 'The weighted average cost of capital, perfect capital markets and project life: a clarification', *Journal of Financial and Quantitative Analysis*, **15**, 3, 719–30.

Miles, J. A. and Ezzell, J. R. (1985) 'Reformulating tax shield valuation: a note', *Journal of Finance*, **40**, 5, 1485–92.

Miller, M. (1988) 'The Modigliani-Miller propositions after thirty years', *Journal of Economic Perspective*, **2**, 99–120.

Mills, R., (1998) *The use of shareholder value analysis in acquisitions and divestment decisions by large UK companies*, CIMA Research Series, ISBN 1859713297, 9781859713297

Modigliani, F. and Miller, M. (1958) 'The cost of capital, corporation finance, and the theory of investment', *American Economic Review*, **48**, 261–97.

Miller, M.H. and Modigliani, F. (1961) Dividend Policy, Growth, and the Valuation of Shares. The Journal of Business, 34, 411-433. http://dx.doi.org/10.1086/294442

Modigliani, F. and Miller, M. (1963) 'Corporate income taxes and the cost of capital: a correction', *American Economic Review*, **53**, 3, 433–43.

Myers, S. C. (1974) 'Interactions of corporate financing and investment decisions - implications for capital budgeting', *Journal of Finance*, March, Reprinted in C.F. Lee, ed., Financial Analysis and Planning, Reading, MA: Addison-Wesley, 1982.

Ohlson, J. A. (1995) 'Earnings, equity book values, and dividends in equity valuation', *Contemporary Accounting Research*, **11**, 661–87.

Owen, G. W. (2013) '"Integrated reporting" - A review of developments and implications for the accounting curriculum', *Journal of Accounting Education*, (Special Edition on Sustainability, Sept 2013).

Rutterford, J. (2000) 'The cost of capital and shareholder value', *Value-based Management. Context and Application*, Wiley Chichester.

Sharpe, W. F. (1964) 'Capital asset prices: a theory of market equilibrium under conditions of risk', *Journal of Finance*, **XIX**, 3, 425–42.

Treynor, J. L. (1961) *Market Value, Time, and Risk*, Unpublished manuscript, No. 95–209.

Williams, J.B. (1938) *The Theory of Investment Value*. Cambridge, MA: Harvard University Press.

Postscript
How to Value a Company:
A Step-by-Step Methodology

Introduction

Company valuation is an exact science using uncertain data. Many methods have been developed in the past 100 years, all differently described and packaged, but one fact is irrefutable; intrinsic valuation is fundamentally based on expectations of future cash flows discounted by a rate of return known as 'cost of capital'. This 'hurdle rate' compensates investors for sacrificing their ability to invest their money immediately in an alternative investment and having to wait for their returns from the investment made. This discount rate is called the 'opportunity cost' and represents the rate of return the investor would expect to earn in the next best alternative investment of equivalent financial and market risk.

This postscript will demonstrate a systematic method for valuing a company

The initial discount rate to be calculated will be Ke_g or the geared cost of equity. It has already been explained earlier in this book that it is unnecessary to use the weighted average cost of capital (WACC) as this is an irrelevance in the equity valuation process. In practical terms, the logical starting point would be to calculate the ungeared cost of capital (Ke_u), but in practice, this requires the equity beta to be ungeared using the formula immediately below and then used in the CAPM equation to determine Ke_U, which using the following formula, creates a circular argument. This is due to needing to already know the debt/equity ratio when the intrinsic value of the company's equity is what ultimately needs to be estimated*:

Ungeared beta = Geared beta/(1 + ((1 - t$_R$)/debt-to-equity ratio)*

The method used here addresses the above circularity problem in ungearing the beta when a geared equity beta has already been calculated from past data. The method of doing so involves using the observed historical equity beta to establish the company's geared required rate of return, using the CAPM model. The next step is to directly ungear the cost of equity using Equation (10) in Chapter 1 to determine the ungeared cost of capital (Ke$_U$) and then, using Equation (16) formulated in Chapter 4, adopt the modified APV method to discount the expected future cash flows of the company, incorporating a constant growth factor and adjusting for tax.

Variables required for valuing a company

There are eight base variables required to calculate the present value of a company from a normative perspective. These are as follows:

1. Obtain the geared equity beta of a company from measuring the covariance of past returns (or the slope of company returns to market returns) to equity shareholders of that company over a past period—say two years. How this can be done is shown, as an example for demonstration purposes, below:

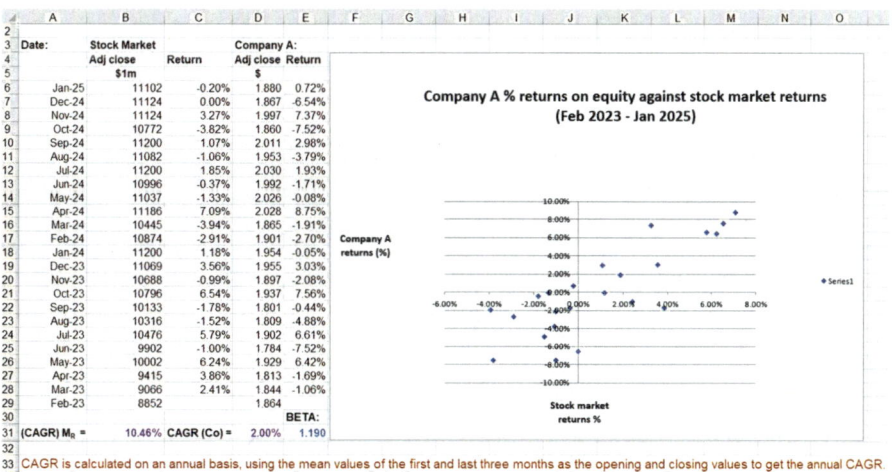

In the above spreadsheet, the percentage changes in returns of the stock market for 24 months are listed in the 3rd column based on the percentage change in the index each month. In the 5th column, the percentage changes in the share price of Company A are shown each month. The beta value is established by calculating the slope of Company A returns against the stock market returns and the market rate of return is calculated using the compound periodic growth rate (CPGR) over two years.

The formula in cell E31 contains the beta calculation and is calculated as follows:

= SLOPE (E6:E28, C6:C28)

where the monthly % changes in Company A's share price are entered as E6:E28 and then the monthly % changes in the stock market index are then entered as C6:C28.

2. Identify the historical mean market rate of return for the stock market in which the company is listed. This is the average return of the market for the period in question as included in cell B31. This would have to be obtained by averaging the returns of all quoted companies in the given stock market over the same period of time which was used to establish the equity beta and this was calculated using the CPGR as follows:

CPGR = (opening stock market value/closing stock market value)$^{1/n}$
where periods are years to determine the annual market rate of return.

3. Identify the value of debt invested in the company (aggregate of all long-term finance)
4. Establish the risk-free rate of return on debt
5. Establish the required mean rate of return of lenders on all borrowed funds including financial instruments and leases (this can be estimated as total finance costs divided by long-term finance outstanding)
6. Establish the marginal rate of business tax
7. Estimate the annual future cash flows before interest and tax into perpetuity

8. Estimate a reasonable constant growth factor for the future cash flows, based on past growth in average cash flows or returns over a given period as calculated in cell D31.

There are then only 3 stages required for establishing the intrinsic market value of equity in a company

1. Calculate the required rate of return for the company (empirical geared cost of equity) by using the equity beta (calculated in the table above) in the following CAPM formula:

$Ke_g = (R_f + (\beta_e \times (M_R - R_f))$

where R_f = risk-free rate of return, β_e = equity beta and M_R = historic market rate of return.

2. Ungear the Ke_g obtained from the CAPM equation to find Ke_U, using Equation (10) from Chapter 1.
3. Use Equation (16) from Chapter 4 to calculate the present value of the company.

This is now demonstrated using the following, based on previous figures used in this book

Company A:

1. Equity beta of the geared Company A: $\beta_e = 1.19$ (as calculated in the spreadsheet above)
2. Historical mean market rate of return for the stock market in which Company A is listed:

$M_R = 10.46\%$ from the spreadsheet calculation of CPGR above

3. Value of debt invested in Company A (aggregate of all long-term finance): $d = \$1m$

4. Risk-free rate of return on debt: $Rf_R = 5\%$ obtained by benchmarking Treasury yields or stable government bond rates.
5. Mean rate of return (cost) of all company borrowing: $K_d = 7\%$
6. Marginal rate of business tax: $t_R = 30\%$
7. Annual future cash flows before interest and tax into perpetuity: $c = \$300,000$
8. Constant growth is estimated at 2% from the spreadsheet above.

Valuation solution

1. Calculate the empirical geared cost of equity (Ke_g) by using the CAPM formula as follows:

$Ke_g = R_f + (\beta_e \times (M_R - R_f))$
$Ke_g = 0.05 + (1.19 \times (0.1046 - 0.05))$
$Ke_g = 0.115$

2. Ungear Ke_g using Equation (10) from Chapter 1:

$Keu = c \times Ke_g / (d \times (Ke_g - K_d) + c)$
$= 300,000 \times 0.115 / (1,000,000 \times 0.045 + 300,000)$
$= 34,500 / (45,000 + 300,000)$
$= 10\%$

3. Calculate the present value of equity using Equation (16) from Chapter 4:

$PV_e = ((c \times (1 + g)/Keu - g)) - d) \times (1 - t_R)$
$= ((300,000 \times (1 + 0.02)/0.1 - 0.02)) - 1,000,000) \times (1 - 0.3)$
$= ((306,000/0.08) - 1,000,000) \times 0.7$
$= 2,825,000 \times 0.7$
$= \$1,977,500$